Catch Your Kids Before They Fall

They Fall

140+
Skill-Builders
to Boost
Academic
Success

Laureen Reynolds

Crystal Springs
SDE BOOKS

a division of Staff Development for Educators
Peterborough, New Hampshire

Published by Crystal Springs Books
A division of Staff Development for Educators (SDE)
10 Sharon Road, PO Box 500
Peterborough, NH 03458
1-800-321-0401
www.SDE.com/crystalsprings

Published 2010
Printed in the United States of America
14 13 12 11   2 3 4 5

ISBN: 978-1-934026-83-0

Library of Congress Cataloging-in-Publication Data

Reynolds, Laureen, 1969-
  Catch your kids before they fall : 140+ skill-builders to boost
academic success / Laureen Reynolds.
      p. cm.
  Includes bibliographical references and index.
  ISBN 978-1-934026-83-0
  1. Education, Elementary—Activity programs. 2. Education,
Elementary--Parent participation. 3. Academic achievement. I. Title.

LB1592.R49 2010
  372.13--dc22

2010006639

Editor: Sandra J. Taylor
Art Director and Designer: S. Dunholter
Production Coordinator: Deborah Fredericks
Illustrator: Joyce Rainville

Contents

Introduction

Success in school is something we want for every child, every day. The bad news is that as educators we are finding that fewer children are coming to school prepared for success because they have poor muscle development, low oral language capacities, underdeveloped visual systems, and limited knowledge of literacy and numeracy concepts. In addition, today's teachers are facing classrooms full of children who have a wide range of language, cultural, socioeconomic, and family diversity. Some days it's enough to make you want to run. How can we possibly teach to all of these readiness levels and developmental needs, catch up kids who haven't had exposure at home to key concepts, and sculpt the classroom landscape to ensure that every student has appropriate opportunities for success? For starters, read this book.

Each chapter in *Catch Your Kids Before They Fall* reflects the latest research about and importance of a specific area of learning or development considered crucial to immediate and future school success. In addition to the many ideas and activities for boosting academic success, the book reinforces the philosophy that prevention is better than remediation and that early, purposeful, specific, informed instruction and intervention are the best ways to help all children achieve success.

You may already be familiar with some of the ideas mentioned above if your school is developing a Response to Intervention (RTI) framework and working toward data-based decision-making to improve instructional practices and individual achievement. This book helps you there too. With simple assessment checklists to help guide your instruction, ideas for interventions that address specific areas of deficiency, and plenty of research to support them, this book supports the paradigm shift occurring in many schools because of the reauthorization of IDEA and NCLB legislation. It also aims to cause a shift in our thinking as educators and to offer a different perspective on teaching: that sometimes going forward means going backward first, and that meeting children where they are is the best way to move them ahead.

Increasing student success is not about adding more time to the day. Longer days, weeks, or years will not make our students more successful—better teaching will. More effective, responsive teaching, purposeful planning for the whole child, noticing and embracing children's differences, paying attention to pieces we've traditionally skipped over, employing best practices, and using the research that has determined what all kids need and offers insight into how the brain learns best—all these will help us help them succeed.

Every teacher's heart wishes for a few things in a good resource book: readable research (√), practical strategies (√), ideas that can be used with any group size (√), suggestions that tie into state standards and required curricula (√), and activities that can be done easily with materials that we already have (√). That's all right here in one place. By doing any of the activities in this book, you will address more areas of skill and development than just those you had your sights set on. The pathways to school success are so intertwined that it's almost impossible not to.

Before you begin reading the following chapters, review the general questions on pages 125–126 in the Study Guides. Then start reading this book anywhere you want—the beginning isn't always the best place. The best place is the one that will help you move your students toward success.

CHAPTER 1

Gross Motor Skills: Don't Leave Home Without Them

Gross motor skills are those needed to control the body's large muscles. These muscles allow children to lift, walk, reach, run, jump, sit, hop, etc., and are essential for maintaining balance and coordination. The National Association for Sport and Physical Education recommends that children in preschool and the primary grades get about two hours of physical activity each day in order to be at optimal readiness for learning. Also, they should not be still for more than 60 minutes at a time outside of school (unless they're sleeping, of course).

When we are trying to improve a child's gross motor skills, we need to be sure to address their body awareness (where their body is in space), their motor planning (figuring out how to do a new task like climbing), their ability to cross the vertical midline of the body (left hand to right knee) and use both sides of the body during an activity, and their locomotor skills (how many ways they can travel—walk, run, jump, etc.).

While gross motor skills involve mostly large muscle groups, it's crucial to remember that the development of the large muscles will ultimately determine how successful a child will be when it comes to using his small muscles for actions like tying shoes, buttoning clothing, cutting, and writing.

Children need to have basic gross motor abilities before they can advance to more complex movements. If students are struggling to do something, simplify the task and see if they are more successful. Success will lead them toward developing better skills. Children's gross motor muscle development should be targeted on a regular basis and as early as possible.

What the Experts Say and Why It Matters

- Children who watch too much TV and video entertainment develop gross motor skills more slowly.

- Students with poor motor development may have difficulties with school-based activities, such as writing at their desks or on the board, sitting in their chairs, or sitting up during circle time on the rug.

- Children who can't use their large muscles skillfully have difficulty sitting still and staying focused on hand-eye activities like reading and writing.

- The ability to maintain an upright sitting posture without using arms for balance or support requires sufficient shoulder and trunk strength.

- Pushing a child to do a task that is impossible because of muscle development status leads to frustration and disappointment, and promotes a lack of self-esteem and self-control.

- If a child's awareness of her body in space is not well developed, the ability to read and write effectively is compromised, as the small motor muscles will not work well together.

- If a child is not able to cross the midline of his body, he will struggle with letter and word orientation and possibly letter reversals, which could result in his being labeled learning disabled or dyslexic.

- Engaging students in balance activities creates a more effective communication system in their brains.

- In order for information to be processed efficiently, it needs to be processed on both sides of the brain.

- In order for children to reach their full potential, learning must be directly connected to physical movement. Discovering three-dimensional space and mastering it through movement enables children to learn valuable concepts that apply to mathematics, reading, and writing.

- As a child grows older, the opportunities for developing motor control lessen, thus reducing the strength of the connections in his brain.

Encouraging Development in This Area
Building Body Awareness

Body awareness is just what it sounds like—the ability to know where one's body is in relation to the objects in one's environment. It allows us to sit down without constantly staring at the chair or to dress without looking directly at our clothing, for example. Children need body awareness so they can keep a comfortable distance from other people, sit in their chairs without falling out, walk fluidly, stand in line, and perform many other tasks we associate with school and life. Children who have poor body awareness might appear clumsy or disorganized. They may have trouble moving without looking at their body, repeatedly break crayons or pencils while using them, or be unable to climb on playground equipment. Below are some activities to try during your daily classroom routine. You can even include content-area practice while you and your students engage in some of these.

Move & Sing

Play an action-based song for your students (two well-known examples are "The Wheels on the Bus" and the "Hokey Pokey"). Make up actions to go with different parts of the song ahead of time or with your students just before you play it. Model these first and give children a chance to practice the motions without the music. Then play the song and encourage students to move the way they practiced.

Simon Says

Play the traditional version but be sure to have students imitate large movements, like rotating their arms at the shoulders, pretending to kick a ball, or galloping. Another variation is to say something like, "If 2 + 2 is 4, then Simon says stomp your left foot," or "If cake and bake rhyme, Simon says shrug your shoulders."

Ribbons Go 'Round

Supply students with short dowels that have a ribbon stapled or taped to the end of each one. Ask them to spread out so there's plenty of room between them and allow them some time to do random movements. Then give them specific instructions, such as "Make clockwise circles with your ribbon," "Spin your ribbon over your head four times," "Make the letter *a* in the air with your ribbon," "Write the word *the* in the air," and so on.

Ready, Set, Action

Make a copy of the spinner reproducible on page 108, adding or taking away sections as needed. Laminate the spinner (or spinners, if you're placing children in small groups). Then write an action word in each section. Attach a paper clip to the center with a brass fastener. The teacher or a designated person spins the spinner by flicking the paper clip, reads the word it lands on, and leads the whole class in that action. This can be used just for fun, but it can also help get the wiggles out before a story is read or serve as an engaging introduction or reinforcement to a lesson on verbs.

Calling All Bodies

This is a great body awareness activity. In addition to developing balance, it builds oral vocabulary, reinforces the concept of left and right, and since many of the tasks require children to cross their midlines, helps establish hand dominance. Ask students to stand apart from each other (so they have room to move safely) on your rug area or outside. Then give them body-part-to-body-part instructions, such as "Move your right elbow to your left knee" or "Touch your left thumb to your right ear."

Charades

Have a student act out an animal movement, a daily activity, or a chore, and whoever guesses correctly becomes the next actor. If desired, make task cards with pictures that students can choose from, showing, for example, vacuuming, hanging clothes, raking, getting dressed, cooking, shoveling snow, and other motions that involve their entire bodies.

Beanbag Heads

Have children place beanbags on their heads and move around the room. The object is simply to keep their bags on their heads. If you wish, you can have students practice skip counting, reciting the alphabet, or something similar as they move. Allow children to try this on a balance beam, on a tape line on the floor, or on the curbing on a sidewalk (with adult supervision). You can also incorporate locomotor tasks like walking heel to toe or walking backward while trying to keep the beanbag in place.

Obstacle Courses

Set up obstacle courses indoors or out, but be sure to model how to complete the course safely. Use crawling tunnels, footprint paths, hanging bars, balance boards or beams, chairs, or mini-trampolines. As a student travels from one obstacle to the next, she can tap a balloon to keep it in the air, sky-write lazy eights (sideways figure eights), dribble a basketball with alternate hands, juggle one ball from hand to hand, or travel using different actions, like shuffling her feet, galloping, or skipping.

Follow the Yellow Brick Road

Tape yellow index cards or pieces of paper to the floor in a random but walkable pattern. Play music and have students follow the road, stepping only on the yellow "bricks." When you stop the music, children stop, turn in the opposite direction, and wait for the music to begin again. Then they move until you stop the music again. If desired, include shapes or numbers on the cards that the students need to identify orally as they go along.

Hopping & Jumping

Ask students to hop on one foot and then both feet, hop backward or sideways, or hop over obstacles. You can also tape a pathway of paper lily pads or something similar to the floor and write sight words on each one. As students hop along the path, they must read each word. Jumping jacks work well here, too. Students can count, or recite a sequence like the months of the year, as they jump. Another option is the kangaroo hop, where each child holds something small like a ball or an orange between her knees and jumps forward, backward, and sideways with feet together. Some students may need a larger object to start out with or to practice just holding it between their knees before an action is added.

Marching Ants

The Ants Go Marching is a favorite playground game I've used with children for years. They love it and it allows me to do a little informal assessment of their gross motor skills. In this game, students pretend they are a line of ants traveling to a picnic. The rules are simple: they need to stay in line (single file) as they follow the leader, look out for each other, and move safely. You may need to review your expectations for the use of playground equipment. The leader (you) holds a dowel with a ribbon attached and this directs the ants' movements. So if you want your line of ants to go through a crawling tunnel, wave your ribbon over it (you don't actually have to crawl through yourself, unless you want to!). The ants crawl through the tunnel and as they begin to emerge from the other end, you lead them on to the next obstacle.

Motor Planning

Motor planning involves thinking about how you are going to move your body to accomplish a task. We do it all the time. Much motor planning is subconscious (how fast to move, with how much force, at what moment), but if you've ever undertaken a new task and had to stop and think about how to get your body to do it, that was motor planning. Children's brains are involved with this planning every day because many actions are still new to them. If children are having difficulty with motor planning, they might appear clumsy; grip objects like pencils and crayons awkwardly; have difficulty jumping, running, and dancing or show resistance to engaging in those activities; or watch to see how others approach a motor task before trying it themselves.

There are some simple accommodations you can make for children who seem to be having difficulty with motor planning skills. Give one direction at a time, use visual cues, have students echo-chant directions, model for them how to complete a motor action, break the task down into smaller parts, and minimize distractions in the room. Even simple things like challenging children to get up from the rug without using their hands can strengthen these large muscles quickly and be repeated many times in a day.

Madcap Motor Moves

Give students a sequence of gross motor movements to do, starting with one task and adding others, one at a time. For example, ask them to put their hands on their heads. Then, with their hands on their heads, ask them to hop on one foot. Next, with hands on heads and hopping on one foot, they spin around, and so forth. "My Aunt Came Back" is a perfect song to accompany this.

Casting Call

Ask students to act out new information they are learning at school (like how a boa constrictor coils around its prey). To act like someone or something other than themselves, they will need to think about what to make their bodies do. Have them try unfamiliar activities too, like driving a car, conducting an orchestra, or directing traffic.

Future Architects of America

Provide students with plenty of opportunities to play with construction toys like Legos, building blocks, and Lincoln logs during free choice, at centers, or any other time that fits your routine. Such play works large muscles in the shoulders and trunk.

Mix It Up

Ask students to eat their snacks or lunches with their nondominant hand. This requires motor planning even for adults, so it's a great stretch for a child's brain. Suggest to parents that they have their children use their nondominant hand to brush their teeth or their hair, to operate the remote control or computer mouse, or to open doors or drawers. Please remember not to ask children to write or cut with their nondominant hand at this stage, however, as they are just beginning to establish their hand preference for those more complicated tasks.

Body vs. Balloon

Have students hit a balloon in the air or back and forth with a classmate by striking it with different parts of their bodies. You might call out "right knee three times" or "left pinky finger twice." This helps students with left-right discrimination as well as motor planning.

Crossing the Midline and Coordinating Both Sides of the Body

Many daily activities require children to use both sides of their bodies at the same time—sometimes each side is doing the same thing (pulling on a sock), and sometimes each side is doing something different (writing). When we encourage children to cross the midline of their bodies, we are actually enabling the brain to construct pathways that will help children with their reading, writing, and mathematical learning later. A child who has difficulty crossing the midline might turn his entire body to look at something, move his whole body instead of his hand and arm when writing or tracing, and display few lead-assist skills where one hand is dominant in a task and the other is supportive (writing and cutting). He may also switch hands during cutting, writing, and coloring tasks and reach for objects with the closest hand instead of reaching across his body to get or place something.

A Whole Lotta Jumpin' Goin' On

Give students tasks to perform while they are doing a variety of movements, such as:

- Have them do jumping jacks while they recite the months of the year.
- Ask them to jump and land with their feet apart as they read a sight word, and then jump and land with feet together as they repeat the sight word.
- Supply each child with a jump rope and ask her to count while jumping. If she misses a jump, she starts counting and jumping from where she began (1 or 2, 5, 10, etc., if skip counting).
- Have students draw a hopscotch path of their choice and then write letters, numbers, or words in each square. As they hop onto each square, they say the letter, number, or word written there.

Bounce, Catch & Kick

Give students playground balls and ask them to bounce theirs in front of them, catching it each time after one bounce. Then ask them to dribble the ball with alternating hands. Finally, have them lightly kick the ball in small increments within a proscribed space. You can add a counting regimen if you wish: for each bounce, dribble, or kick, they progress the count.

Beanbag Toss & Target Practice

Supply each student with a beanbag. Ask them to practice throwing their beanbags in the air with one hand and catching them with the other. Next have them take steps forward as they do this, and then backward. Finally, establish a target area (spots marked on the wall or boxes on the floor) and ask students to throw their beanbags at their designated spots or into their designated boxes, retrieve them, and repeat the exercise 10 times.

Keep the Beat

Borrow some rhythm sticks from your music teacher, or use new, unsharpened pencils, and challenge children to keep up with the beat you create. For example, you might repeat a pattern of tapping your sticks together twice in front of you and then once above your head, or tapping them once behind your back, moving them in a circle over your head, and then tapping them once more in front of you. Model this for your students and encourage them to join in when they are ready.

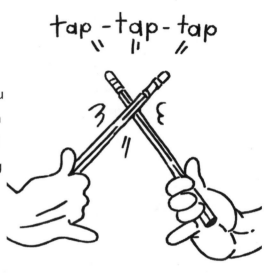

Do the Locomotion

Skipping or marching, shuffling or sliding, walking on heels or toes—all are great ways to build the big muscles. Have your students gather in a circle and tell them that when you say "Go!" they are to turn to their right and start skipping in a circle until you give the next command. Then explain that when you say "Stop, turn, march," they are to stop skipping, turn to their left, and march in the circle, going in the opposite direction, until you give them the next command. Another direction might be "Stop, turn, shuffle," and so forth.

Art Works

While we may consider art projects fine-motor muscle developers (and they are!), think about how many times during the course of completing a project a child needs to cross his midline or coordinate both sides of his body to get the job done (cutting, gluing, placing, tearing, tracing, etc.). Students can create seasonal or monthly craft projects like valentines for February or construction-paper flowers for May. They can also do art projects connected to science or social studies content, like molding dinosaurs out of clay or creating dioramas in shoe boxes to show a particular habitat or a scene from the life of a famous person.

Quick Hits

Other self-explanatory gross motor goodies include "hiding" one arm behind the back and using the other to retrieve objects, opening snack or lunch containers, including zip-top plastic bags, and sharpening pencils manually.

Where Should Kids Be?

Assessment Checklist – 4 years

	Yes	No
Throws ball underhand with accuracy		
Catches large ball from 5 feet away using body and hands		
Hops on one foot one time		
Balances on one foot briefly		
Jumps a short distance forward and backward		
Bounces ball accurately		
Kicks a still ball		
Alternates feet on stairs		
Runs around obstacles		
Runs on tiptoes		

Additional Notes

_____

_____

_____

_____

Assessment Checklist – 5 years

	Yes	No
Throws ball in air and catches it		
Gets up without using hands		
Bounces and catches ball		
Balances on one foot for at least 5 seconds		
Walks on a line, heel to toe		
Walks on tiptoes		
Runs with arms swinging in opposition to feet		
Walks backward		
Pumps on swing, unsustained (can pump once or twice but can't sustain swinging motion)		
Hops on preferred foot for a short distance		

Additional Notes

_____

_____

_____

_____

Assessment Checklist – 6 years

	Yes	No
Throws and catches small ball with accuracy		
Kicks a rolling ball		
Dribbles a ball		
Jumps rope		
Pumps on a swing to sustain motion		
Moves in time to a beat or rhythm		
Walks easily on balance beam		
Catches ball with hands only		
Skips		
Gallops		

Additional Notes

_____

_____

_____

_____

_____

Home-School Connection

Dear Parent/Guardian,

I know that each of you wants your child to be as successful as possible in school and that you already know there are many things your child needs to practice, such as reading, writing, and math concepts. But did you know that one of the greatest predictors of a child's success in school is the development of their gross motor skills? It's true. The muscles that help us sit up, walk, and jump are the foundation for the rest of the learning we do. The physical movements associated with developing these large muscles cause our brains to become stronger and more efficient. To help your child get these muscles working, have him or her try some of these activities:

- Wring out wet sponges in the bathtub or when washing the car—water play is great!

- Use a manual can opener.

- Play tag or chase but have child hop, waddle, or dance instead of run.

- Hammer nails or pegs.

- Use sidewalk chalk.

- Write or draw on a chalkboard, easel, or paper taped to the wall.

- Participate in cooking activities, such as mixing by hand or kneading dough.

- Shuffle and deal cards during card games.

- Dry silverware with a dish towel.

- Watch TV (rainy days only!) while propped up on elbows.

- Catch and kick different-sized balls.

- Move in various ways to music (hop, jump, skip, slither).

- Be a human wheelbarrow (hold up their legs as they walk on their hands).

- Walk along a curb (with adult supervision).

- March, skip, or hop through the neighborhood with you.

- Toss and catch a small ball or beanbag while lying down or sitting, using alternating hands.

- Crawl through a cardboard box or playground tunnels.

- Build an indoor obstacle course together using pillows, chairs, or cushions, or an outdoor course, using items you have in the yard or on the patio. Then have your child navigate the course.

- Walk on a balance beam made from a strip of tape or string laid on the floor.

- Dance to movement songs like "I'm a Little Teapot."

You don't need to do all of these—just make sure your child uses his or her large muscles each day.

Sincerely,

CHAPTER 2

Fine Motor Skills Matter, Too

Fine motor skills can be defined as small muscle movements in the wrists, hands, and fingers in coordination with the eyes. These skills are required to tie shoes, fasten and unfasten buttons, pick up small objects, and point to something. Children also need them to hold a pencil, cut with scissors, turn pages in a book, manipulate a computer mouse, and write.

Fine motor control is the coordination of muscles, bones, and brain power to produce precise motion. It requires an awareness of hands and fingers as well as motor planning (figuring out how you're going to go about doing a new motor task). Fine motor skills develop more slowly than gross motor skills, so the process requires more patience from children and the adults teaching them. It also takes lots of practice—hours of playing in, exploring, and physically manipulating one's environment.

Young children spend approximately 70 percent of their time engaged in fine motor work or activities. Developing proficiency in fine motor control allows the child to develop skills that will have positive outcomes immediately and in later life. Early on, fine motor skills help children grasp things and begin to care for themselves (comb their hair, brush their teeth). Later, well-developed fine motor muscles will aid a child with drawing, coordination, hand-eye control, handwriting, reading, playing a musical instrument, keyboarding, sports, and more. Fine motor muscles within the eyes help students track print as they read, copy from the board, and identify letters, numbers, and words.

You can see how important these little muscles are and why we can't delay in developing them in our children. The optimal time for building fine motor skills (according to brain research) is 6 months to 8 years, so we need to get busy. As you go through the activities in the pages that follow, watch for children having difficulty with fine motor tasks. Take a step back and simplify tasks or break them down into smaller steps. You may also want to consider whether a child has the large muscle development that is a precursor to the activity (see Chapter 1, page 6). No matter how you approach the development of fine motor skills, make certain of one thing—that it's fun for the child.

What the Experts Say and Why It Matters

- Children who don't spend thousands of hours cutting, coloring, drawing, playing with puzzles, etc., will not fully develop hand-eye and near-point (16 inches or less from the face) visual skills—the skills necessary to read and write with ease.

- Children with poor fine motor skills usually have trouble with visual memory, an important skill for remembering how words look; reading, printing, and spelling; and understanding basic number concepts.

- Inadequate fine motor development can cause embarrassment and a lack of self-confidence in children. These in turn can affect their academic performance for the rest of their years in school.

- The more time children spend exploring their environment independently and with others, the more their brains develop. With every small physical interaction, new connections are being made in the brain, strengthening the learning network.

- The fine motor skills children use when they explore their environments help them make judgments later on about objects and situations without needing physical contact.

- Children with poor fine motor skills complete less work and must work harder to complete most tasks.

- Poor fine motor skills have the potential to limit children's career choices later in life.

- When actions are not automatic, the available working memory and attentional space in the brain is taken up with concentrating on the movement rather than the concept being learned and practiced.

Encouraging Development in This Area

Building Blocks

Learning how to cut, draw, color, efficiently grip a pencil, and print—all share the same foundation of fine motor skills. Completing these and other fine motor tasks, like dressing and feeding oneself, require the wrists, hands, and fingers to do lots of different actions. Building the muscles in the hands will result in the least fatiguing, most pleasurable fine motor experiences for children. Go through your lesson plans with a purposeful eye: are there opportunities to use these muscle builders in activities you already plan to do? Most likely there are many, but here are a few more to consider.

The All-Important Arches

The ability to arch the hands allows for the most efficient, least fatiguing pencil grip. To ensure that your children are developing the small muscles needed for this, involve them in activities such as the following:

- Give them a small, round object to roll in their palms, such as a marble, rubber ball, or golf ball; or pinch off a portion of Play-Doh and have them roll it into a ball in their palms, mash it flat between their palms, and roll it into a ball again.

- Ask them to roll a pair of dice with both hands cupped.

- Have them line up pennies or bingo chips and then turn them over as fast as possible.

- Give each a zip-top plastic bag and let them open and close it repeatedly.

- Ask them to hold their cupped hands together while you pour uncooked rice, elbow macaroni, or dried beans into their hands until they can hold no more.

Wrist Strengtheners

Wrist stability helps keep pencils and scissors moving fluidly and contributes to the quality of handwriting. It also helps children feed themselves without spilling. Strengthen children's wrists with the following activities:

- Give them rolling pins and have them flatten clay or dough or crush crackers into fine crumbs. Make sure they keep their hands open as they use the rolling pins, not closed around the end handles.

- Have them place toys on vertical shelves, or paint, draw, or color on paper mounted on a wall or other vertical surface.

- Let them play with windup toys or music boxes that need to be rewound. This develops the ability to turn the palm up or down.

Touch Control

Delicate touch is the ability to use different amounts of pressure for different tasks. For example, a delicate touch keeps us from ripping the paper when we are writing or erasing. Many children do not have a good sense of this, as you know if you've ever looked right through their papers! Here are some fun ways for them to practice touch control:

- Ask children to pick up fragile items like cereal flakes or minimarshmallows with their fingers or tweezers—without breaking the flakes or denting the marshmallows.

- Pass out tracing or tissue paper and ask children to draw or write on it without tearing or puncturing their piece.

- Have children line up dominoes on their ends or release drops of water from an eyedropper one drop at a time.

Finger Practice

Individual finger movements are also important in almost all fine motor tasks. Engage children with pointing games, finger puppets, finger plays, finger painting, fingerprinting, pasting, toy telephones or pianos, poking bubbles, and keyboard exercises.

Opposition

Opposition means touching a finger to the thumb. This ability enables us to do things like button, snap, zip, or move small objects. To develop and strengthen this, children can play with turkey basters or eyedroppers at a water table; paint pictures using eyedroppers; pick up small objects like raisins, marbles, or round cereal; insert and pull pegs out of a peg board; pull and pinch pieces of dough or clay; put coins into a piggy bank or slots; flick something off the thumb with each finger; or attach and remove clothespins from the edge of a coffee can or shoe box.

Unilateral/Bilateral

Unilateral hand skills (using one hand) and bilateral hand skills (using two hands together) help children build dominant hand strength and cross the midline of their bodies—critical skills for reading and writing fluency, among other things. Build unilateral hand skills by having children stack blocks to build a tower, drive a toy car along a strip of tape on the floor or a table, play with peg boards, throw a ball or beanbag at a target, catch a ball or beanbag with a scoop, and hit a suspended ball with the hand or a paddle. Bilateral skills can be developed through rhythm games that involve clapping and tapping sticks or cymbals; playing with pop beads or blocks that connect; scooping sand, beans, or rice with two hands; holding a clothes basket or box and catching a ball in it; using a rolling pin to flatten cookie dough or clay; rolling, throwing, or catching a large ball with two hands; pushing or carrying large objects with two hands; or hitting a suspended ball with a soft bat.

Pre-Printing Skills

Pre-printing skills enable a child to create the strokes necessary to make letters and numbers. The foundation for skills needed for pre-printing is actually based in both gross and fine motor muscles and includes posture and balance, adequate shoulder strength, hand and arm control, pencil grip, two-hand usage, and hand-eye coordination. In other words, for a child to be successful at the pre-printing stage, she needs to have gross motor and some fine motor development already in place. It's not just about the hands (a common misconception); it's also about the prerequisite skills and muscle development.

The general progression of pre-printing skills is as follows:

Random scribble

Circular scribble

Scribble in a horizontal or vertical direction

Imitate then copy a vertical or horizontal line

Imitate then copy a cross

Imitate and copy diagonal lines

Imitate and copy a square

Imitate and copy a triangle

Imitate and copy a diamond

(Note: In this context, "imitate" means that a child watches an adult draw something and then attempts to draw the same thing; "copy" means that an adult shows a child a picture of something and asks her to draw the same thing, but without any demonstration. Imitation always precedes copying.)

Activities for Developing Pre-Printing Skills

Give your students lots of practice with the following:

- Write or draw with a stick in sand, dirt, or snow.

- Trace over lines or shapes with a finger and then with different-colored markers.

- Use their fingers to trace over a line or shape you create in shaving cream, pudding, salt, or rice.

- Make letters, numbers, lines, or shapes out of tape on the floor, a wall, or a tabletop. Ask children to drive a toy car along the tape.

- Help students stay on a path when tracing with their fingers by gluing pipe cleaners or yarn on both sides of a line or shape.

- Complete dot-to-dot pictures.

- Use simple mazes that reflect the shapes your students are working on.

- Make lines and shapes on a Lite-Brite board.

- Use a chopstick to make shapes and lines in the bottom of a pie tin that has been covered with clay or Play-Doh. Then they smooth out the surface with their fingertips and make another shape.

- Use a hole punch to make shapes and lines in paper.

Getting Their Muscles Ready for Writing

Muscles are like musical instruments; they need to be "tuned" or warmed up before they can be used effectively. So, before asking children to write, you first need to prepare their muscles for the task. Although writing requires work from mostly the smaller muscles, efficient writers also need some of their bigger muscles (like arm and shoulder muscles) to be ready for action. Use the activities below to get their muscles "in shape."

Writing Warm-Ups

If you include handwriting practice at a center, take advantage of the task cards reproducible on page 109. Make copies of the cards, cut them apart, put out the necessary materials, and let children choose a card to determine how they will warm up for writing.

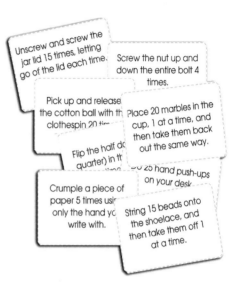

Unscrew and screw the jar lid 15 times, letting go of the lid each time.

Screw the nut up and down the entire bolt 4 times.

Pick up and release the cotton ball with th clothespin 20 ti

Place 20 marbles in the cup, 1 at a time, and then take them back out the same way.

Flip the half d quarter) in th

25 hand push-ups on your desk

Crumple a piece of paper 5 times usir only the hand yo write with.

String 15 beads onto the shoelace, and then take them off 1 at a time.

Little Muscle Movements

Model these activities first to make sure children are doing them correctly.

- Pencil Walk-Ups: Make sure the child is holding his pencil correctly, and then have him walk his fingers from the tip of the pencil up to the eraser and back down again.

- Piano Playing: Tell the child to place her hands flat on her desk and slowly lift up one finger while keeping the rest on the desk. Then, ask her to slowly bring her finger back down to the desk. Have her repeat this with her other fingers.

- Spider Push-Ups: Have the child place his hands on his desk in an arched or cupped position and then push them down.

- Spider Push-Ups on a Mirror: Have the child do the previous exercise, but with both of her hands pressing against each other instead of the desk.

- Trumpet Playing: Tell the child to touch each of his fingers to his thumb, and then reverse the order: thumb to pointer, thumb to middle, thumb to ring, thumb to pinky, and then thumb to ring, thumb to middle, thumb to pointer.

Big Muscle Movements

Model these activities first to make sure children are doing them correctly.

- Washing Machine: Ask the child to stand up, place her hands on her hips, and rotate her body from side to side.

- Chair Push-Ups: Tell the child to sit in his chair, place his hands on the chair on each side of his body, push up his whole body, and then let it down.

- Apple Picking: Using his right hand, the child reaches up for an imaginary apple on his right side, and then turns and bends down to place it in an imaginary basket next to his left foot. Then he uses his left hand to reach up and pick an apple, and places it in the basket at his right foot.

- Windmills: With arms out and elbows straight, the child touches her right hand to her left foot and then her left hand to her right foot, bending at the waist each time.

- Wake-Ups: The child places her arms with elbows straight out to the sides at shoulder level. Then she touches her hands to her shoulders and repeats the exercise.

- Head and Neck Rolls: Have the child slowly roll her head from one side to the other and then back again.

- Desk Push-Downs: Have the child place her hands on her desk with her fingers pointed away from her body. Then she pushes down as hard as she can.

- Shake-Outs: Ask the child to shake different parts of her body—arms, legs, hands, etc.

- Shoulder Shrugs: The child raises his shoulders up toward his ears and then lowers them.

Scissor Skills

Practicing scissor skills also develops pre-printing, pre-reading, and coloring skills. Upon entering kindergarten, children can be expected to use scissors, but only if they've had many hours of practice at home. Cutting is not an assumed skill; it takes practice. Children should be able to cut around corners and along curved lines, and be able to cut out squares and circles. By the end of the kindergarten year, children should also be able to cut out spirals, triangles, and stars.

The general progression of scissor skills is as follows:

Cutting air: squeeze and release to build strength and coordination

Snipping: one cut

Cutting through strips: consecutive snips

Cutting along a straight line

Cutting angles or turning: squares

Cutting along a curved line

Cutting circles

Cutting spirals

Cutting triangles

Cutting simple black-line shapes

Cutting complex shapes with angles, curves, and multiple lines

Activities for Developing Scissor Skills

- Vary the kinds of paper you ask students to cut. Start with heavier stock paper and move to lighter stock as their skills improve.

- When students are in the snipping stage, ask them to cut materials that require a single cut such as straws, yarn, tape, or skinny strips of paper.

- Progress to wider strips or pieces of paper so that consecutive snips are required. The more skilled the child becomes, the wider the paper should be so that more consecutive snips are necessary to cut through it.

- Once children begin to cut lines and shapes, start with wide lines. As accuracy improves, decrease the thickness of the lines. If necessary, lines can be several inches thick at first.

- If children have trouble staying on a cutting path, make lines with glue (and let them dry), or glue yarn or skinny straws like coffee stirrers on each side of the path to guide them.

- Use a hole punch to make holes along the path or practice lines or shapes, and ask students to cut from hole to hole. Increase the distance between the holes as their skills improve.

- In the early stages, trace the shape outline to be cut on a small piece of paper. As children's skills improve, trace the shape on bigger pieces of paper so students need to maneuver the paper more.

- Start with large shapes and decrease size as skills improve.

- Draw simple dot-to-dot pictures and have children cut from dot to dot.

- Have the child lie on the floor, propped up on her elbows, when cutting.

Let Art Do Its Part

Art projects are fun and a natural pathway to developing fine motor muscles, so make art a part of your routine. You will see a dramatic improvement in everything fine motor (and more!).

- Have children tear scraps of construction paper and then glue them onto a sheet of paper to create pictures or abstract art.

- Ask children to trace around their forearms, hands, and fingers to create the trunk and branches of a tree. Slightly crumpled tissue paper squares can be the leaves.

- Children make seasonally colored paper chains to decorate the classroom any time of the year or to practice patterns during math.

- Show children how to fold paper to make hats and airplanes. As their skills improve, show them how to fold and cut paper to make paper doll chains and snowflakes. Folding and cutting provide great practice for fine motor skills.

Where Should Kids Be?

Assessment Checklist – 4 years

	Yes	No
Begins to show hand preference		
Cuts dough or soft clay with cookie cutter		
Strings beads		
Puts tiny objects in small container		
Folds paper without model		
Unscrews and screws a large lid		
Cuts a small piece of paper in two		
Imitates drawing a cross		
Winds a windup toy		
Draws a circle		
Performs simple sewing on a lacing card		
Builds a tower of 7 blocks		
Puts together a simple puzzle		
Holds a pencil		
Places small pegs in holes		
Cuts straight and curvy lines		

Additional Notes

_____

_____

_____

_____

Assessment Checklist – 5 years

	Yes	No
Holds pencil correctly in tripod grip		
Traces letters		
Copies or writes own name		
Holds scissors correctly		
Cuts out simple shapes		
Builds structures with blocks		
Draws a line from one object to another		
Usually uses dominant hand		
Completes inset puzzles		
Writes a few identifiable letters or numbers		
Creases paper with fingers		
Draws diagonal line		
Uses fingers only to write/draw/color		
Draws person with distinguishable parts of the body (head, arms, legs, trunk)		

Additional Notes

_____

_____

_____

_____

Assessment Checklist - 6 years

	Yes	No
Uses efficient pencil grip		
Cuts out complex pictures with accuracy		
Copies sequence of numbers or letters correctly		
Completes complex puzzles		
Buttons, snaps, buckles		
Ties shoes independently		
Writes letters and numbers correctly		
Hand dominance firmly established		
Draws complex, wholly recognizable pictures		
Letters and numbers rest on lines of paper		

Additional Notes

_____

_____

_____

_____

Home-School Connection

Dear Parent/Guardian,

Every year of a child's development brings new and exciting changes. The prime time for brain growth is right now, and one of the best ways to foster it is to put children's fine motor muscles to use. These small muscles of the hands, fingers, and eyes (just to name a few) play an important role in everything your child does, from brushing his or her teeth to reading and writing. Here are some fun, simple things you and your child can do together.

- Fill a container with sand, rice, or water; pour it out, refill it, and repeat.

- Open and close zip-top plastic bags or plastic food-storage containers.

- Use tongs at the dinner table to serve salad.

- Cut a cake into servings and give one piece to each family member; cut tube-style cookie dough before baking.

- Shuffle and deal cards for a family card game; play games like Slap Jack or Concentration.

- Squeeze a spray bottle to help clean a table or windows, or just for fun outside.

- Participate in cooking activities like mixing by hand or kneading dough.

- Play board games that use dice or other manipulatives.

- Do crafts that involve cutting paper or stringing beads, buttons, pasta, etc. to make decorations for different holidays.

- Place coins in a piggy bank slot or flip a coin and keep track of how many times it lands on each side.

- Play board games with spinners or moving pieces.

- Write or draw on a piece of paper taped to the wall.

- Use a baggie filled with ketchup or mustard to practice writing letters and numbers.

- Play tic-tac-toe but use different letters (A and Z instead of X and O, for example).

- Guess what letter or number your child traces on your back and then switch roles.

- Screw and unscrew nuts and bolts.

- Cut pictures out of old greeting cards, cut coupons from the Sunday paper, or cut up junk mail.

- With the dominant hand only, crumple paper to be recycled.

- Remove staples from paper with a staple remover.

As always, these activities provide opportunities for you to share conversations and quality time with your child. Choose those ideas that fit into your daily routine and do them as often as you can. Most of all, have fun!

Sincerely,

CHAPTER 3

Pump Up the Volume on Oral Language Development

The spoken word is the starting point for nearly everything your students will set out to do, both now and in the future. It is the strength that every child possesses, whether she is an English Language Learner, a child from an impoverished background, or a mainstream American student. It's up to us as educators to help our students build a foundation for their future literacy endeavors by talking to them in purposeful ways and encouraging them to talk to us and each other.

We spend a lot of time teaching our students simple words they can use right away and add to their early reading and writing vocabularies. However, we spend very little time ensuring their literacy future by teaching to their almost infinite capacity for developing a strong oral vocabulary—the words they understand when they hear them and use correctly when they speak. These oral vocabularies are often neglected in classrooms at the cost of high-quality conversation, increased listening comprehension, and, later on, writing acumen and reading comprehension.

The diversity in today's classrooms and the advent of a society where parents work longer hours than ever before means that children spend more time with TV and video entertainment and less time in conversations at home. This requires educators to be more proactive about teaching students words that will increase their listening and speaking vocabularies. We need to teach our children sophisticated, meaningful, useful words even before they can read and write. And if we want the best long-term impact possible, if we want to begin to close the achievement gap we see and hear so much about, we need to do it before the end of grade three.

What the Experts Say and Why It Matters

- The larger the oral vocabulary that learners bring to their independent reading, the more likely they are to succeed at their early reading attempts.

- If a child has a strong oral vocabulary already in place, he will have better reading comprehension because by the time he can actually read a particular word, he will already know what it means, even if it's the first time he's read it.

- The size of a child's oral vocabulary at the end of grade one is a significant predictor of reading comprehension ten years later, and may even affect high school dropout rates.

- A strong oral vocabulary in the early years of a child's learning will transform into a formidable writing vocabulary when she begins writing independently.

- A child's ability to accurately describe objects, inform an audience, and relate ideas orally will be reflected in his writing later on and will affect his ability to understand other's descriptions in print.

- Children with strong oral vocabulary skills generally enjoy greater social acceptance.

- In order to understand language at the print level, a child must first understand it at the oral level.

- Developing oral vocabularies will narrow the word-knowledge gap between students from impoverished backgrounds or homes where English is not the primary language and students from mainstream American homes.

- A child who possesses a solid oral vocabulary can follow complex directions more easily than a child who does not.

Encouraging Development in This Area

Start with the Basics

Before you can move on to more sophisticated oral language interactions, you need to be sure that children have the everyday basics firmly planted in their brains. As more children spend more time in poor-quality day care or are raised in homes where parents are too busy to interact, where TV and video entertainment occurs for hours on end, even assumed listening and speaking vocabulary words (basic, everyday words) do not become ingrained. The following suggestions will build the oral language foundation for students who come to school with a weak listening and/or speaking vocabulary.

Shake a Leg

Movement is great for kids for lots of reasons, including helping them develop an action word vocabulary. Several times a day, take a few minutes to do this simple exercise with your students. Ask them to stand up and spread out so they can't touch anybody else. Then tell them to shake their right hand—you should shake yours, too. After 5 seconds, choose another motion, such as patting the knees, stomping the left foot, wiggling the fingers, and so forth. Use a variety of directives, such as "Wave your *opposite* hand" or "Use the *same* foot but move it in a *different* direction." Continue for a few minutes, and then have children go right back to what they were doing previously.

How Are You Feeling Today?

I have a large magnet that is full of bear faces showing many different emotions. I kept it on my filing cabinet, and each day (usually more than once!) a student would ask me how I was feeling. I'd look at the various bear expressions, decide on the appropriate one, and then tell my student. I'd also make a point to reiterate my feeling, scaffolding a little if it was something like "ho-hum," and explain why. Some days I asked students to identify the feeling opposite to the one I was having. It got to the point where my students were nearly knocking each other over to ask me, so we kept track and took turns. Try this or something similar in your classroom, working it into your daily routine wherever it fits. If you have space for a poster near your door, you can do this while kids are in line waiting to go to lunch or recess or to a specialist, and at dismissal time.

Picture Talk

Collect a number of simple pictures from newspapers, magazines, the Internet, or resource books. Hold one up and ask your students a series of questions, such as, "Does anyone know what this is?" "Where might you see something like this?" "What's it used for?" "Who might have one?" "Why would you need one of these?" "What are some words that describe this?" "Is there one in this room?" Continue the conversation as time allows. As you use the pictures, place them in a basket that students have access to during choice time. This will provide opportunities for them to discuss the pictures with each other or offer a personal experience or story that is related. You can also do this during those awkward waiting-in-line times, in guided reading groups, or as an introduction to your language arts block or to a science or social studies concept.

Follow My Directions

Select a picture from a coloring or activity book that depicts something familiar, like a playground, house, animal, or parade. Give a copy to each student, along with specific tasks to do with their crayons that include directional and location words. For example, using a picture of a school, you might ask students to place a green line *under* the front door, a yellow circle *around* the window in the *upper left* corner, a blue X *above* the flagpole, and so on.

Wheel of Words

Using the reproducible on page 108, which can have as many sections as you want, laminate the spinner before you write anything in the sections so it can be reused. In each section, write a question that requires an oral response, and make copies for each group. Display something familiar or unique and invite students to take a turn at the spinner and respond individually or as a group. If the object was a pineapple and the spinner stopped on the section "What does it feel like?" there could be several answers: rough, hard, bumpy, etc. Continue spinning as time allows. It is quite likely that students may not know some of the answers, so supplement and scaffold student responses when necessary. Extend the conversation to include personal experience by asking what kind of food has pineapple in it. If students are old enough to read, make copies of the spinner reproducible and allow them to do the same activity in small, flexible groups, brainstorming and discussing answers as they go.

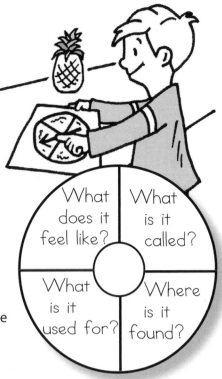

Pass the Plate, Please

Initially, this activity will give students more interesting words to use in their conversations. Ultimately, it will improve their reading comprehension and writing acumen by giving them a broader repertoire of ways to say the same thing. If you are doing this as a whole group, make a giant paper plate out of white poster board. For small groups, use real paper plates and give one to each group. Write an overused word in the middle of the plate, such as *said, big, good, hot, cold, great,* or *small.* Ask students to brainstorm other words with the same meaning and record their answers on the plate. In small groups, each student writes a synonym, then passes the plate to the next student who adds another one. If a group member can't think of a word, she may enlist help from other group members. Each time a plate gets filled up with synonyms, post it in a spot where students can access it easily during writing sessions. It's like a thesaurus on your wall!

Moving on to Something More Sophisticated: Conversations with Peers and Adults

An environment where talking is encouraged is full of learning potential. Hart and Risley state that the most important aspect in evaluating a child care setting is the amount of talk going on, moment by moment, between the children and their caregivers.

Spicing Up Their Speech

If one of your students says to you, "Mrs. Nowell, I really don't get this. I've tried every way I know to find the answer to this problem," you might reply, "Tommy, it sounds to me like you're feeling frustrated because you've attempted everything you know how to do and still can't find the solution. Let's solve it together." In this situation, you've taken Tommy's own words and feelings and repeated them with more sophisticated vocabulary. Chances like this could come up 30 times a day or more—be ready for them!

Teachable, Talkable Moments

When you get a paper turned in with no name on it, hold it up and say, "I've got an anonymous paper here. There's no name on it so I don't know whose it is." When having sophisticated conversations, it is important not only to use new words but also to scaffold them with less complex, kid-friendly explanations.

What's New with You?

To give students opportunities to talk in front of others, ask or answer questions, or respond to comments, build time to share into your class meeting. Students can sign up once a week, if they wish, and share in two or three sentences something that happened, an event they attended, or a piece of news (like "We're getting a cat!"). The child takes three questions or comments from the group, responds to them, and then makes way for the next child who has signed up to share that day.

Conversation Central

Allowing children to talk with each other is important to oral language development. Each child brings a background of some kind to the classroom, and the best way for her to share is, most often, with her voice. Some opportunities for children to chat with each other include sharing and discussing photos provided by families or the teacher, a favorite or familiar book (even if they can't read, they can talk about the pictures), original illustrations, a poster, or a weekend event on a Monday morning.

Using Story Books

As the more literate other, you have the potential to bring rich vocabulary experiences to your children each day. There are more rare words per thousand in children's picture books than in anything else a child will come in contact with, so storybooks are a great resource for sophisticated words. Sharing a story with your students also gives a word a global context that doesn't rely on previous experiences or background knowledge.

A Reading Dress Rehearsal

Before performing on the reading stage, we need to prepare our audience—the children. Pre-reading conversations can set them up for better comprehension and expand their vocabularies, both basic and more sophisticated. A reading dress rehearsal before you read establishes interest in the story. It also reinforces the strategy of relying on visual cues while reading. During a reading dress rehearsal, discuss and predict the possible path of the story by using words and pictures on the book's cover and inside pages, and help children connect the illustrations to their own experiences to activate prior knowledge. Take advantage of opportunities to model thinking out loud, such as, "I see a big tent on this page. I wonder what's going to happen inside." Keep your reading dress rehearsal brief but don't skip it. It's critical for children in your room who have few other literacy experiences each day and valuable for expanding the literacy experiences of those who come with more.

Reading Rhyming Text

Most educators of young children read rhymes with them on a regular basis. If you do, don't stop! If you don't, get going! It is important to share rhyming text (poetry, chants, cheers, books, nursery rhymes) out loud so your students can hear the repeated sounds. It's even more important to share rhyming text and let your students fill in the rhymes out loud as each one comes about.

Referencing Read-Alouds

When reading to young children, it is best to explain a word you want to focus on when you come across it in a story. By doing so you will be supporting their comprehension and giving them an initial reference or context for the word. For the greatest learning potential, revisit the word right after you have finished reading the text. First, remind children how the word was used in the story. After that, explain the meaning of the word again in kid-friendly terms. If the word was *annoyed,* you might explain  it by saying it means to be bugged or bothered by something. Next, relate it to a context different from that of the story where the word was first encountered, perhaps by sharing a personal story (kids love those!) about how annoyed you are when your spouse leaves his socks all over the house. Then ask a few students to share some examples of a time when that word applied to them or someone they know. Claire might share how annoying her younger brother is when he comes into her room even though she has KEEP OUT signs on her door. Calvin might tell the group that his dad gets annoyed when he leaves his toys in the driveway because he runs over them with the car. Sharing personal experiences also starts students on the road to making text-to-self connections when they become independent readers—a strategy that will deepen their comprehension of a text.

Interactive Activities

Getting children to apply actions to and have conversations about vocabulary words can reinforce them better than almost anything else. The more parts of the body used when learning a new idea, the more likely the brain is to remember it. The games that follow are described for a larger group but can easily be adapted for two people like a parent or caregiver and a child.

Ham It Up

After reviewing the meanings of words in other ways, try this activity to get children's faces and bodies into the act. Perhaps your chosen words are *impatient, panicked,* and *crouched.* You could say, "Show me what a parent would look like if she was feeling impatient because you were not ready to go to school." "Show me how you would look if you were feeling panicked because you forgot to study for a spelling test." "Show me how your body would look if you crouched behind a tree during a game of hide-and-seek." You can also ask students to think about what the opposite of each feeling or action might be (*patient, relaxed, standing*) and to show you that as well. Allow children to act out

these words in a group or, with your help, select words from a word bank and play charades. As the most literate person in the group, you should get involved too!

Picture Perfect

This is a simplified version of the popular game Pictionary. It can be played in large or small groups and even pairs. Instead of acting out words, this time children try to draw clues about them. In the beginning, do this activity with the whole group. Gather children on the rug and let the artist use your white board. Give her a word and (secretly) a corresponding illustration or definition, if she needs it. You may want to have a quick conference with her to get her started. Facilitate in any way necessary to ensure success. There is no time limit unless you have older or more able students who want that challenge.

What's on Your Mind?

Play this game to boost basic vocabulary or to expose children to more sophisticated words. Think of an object or a place familiar to your students. If it's an object, try to have one on hand to show the class once the game is over. If it's a local place, take a photo or find a picture that represents a more general scene, like a carnival. Give clues about the object or place and after each one, allow a student to guess. If you are doing this on the basic level, it might be helpful to support each clue with concrete examples such as: the thing that's on my mind is round, just like our classroom globe, or purple like Billy's shirt, or smooth like the tile on the floor, or noisy like our lunchroom, and so on. If what's on your mind rhymes with something, use that as a clue, too. After a certain number of clues, reveal the answer by showing the children either the actual object or the picture of the place you've described. Once they've got the hang of it, allow them to play in pairs or small groups.

Category Clap

Have children sit in a circle. Tell them that you are going to name a category, such as "things related to the desert," and start a clapping beat that your students must follow. While keeping the beat, the first student names something in your category, then the next student adds something else, and so on until everyone has had a chance. Allow children to pass if they wish, but come back to them before you change categories because they may have thought of something as they listened to other children's responses. The goal is to get all the way around the circle without any repeats.

Repeated Exposure

Plan for your students to interact with new words over and over again in different contexts to keep vocabulary acquisition at its peak. It isn't enough to explain a word and then move on; you want to keep going back to the new words every chance you get. The following activities will help do just that.

Photo Finish

Some vocabulary words you choose may lend themselves to an action or an expression. Using a digital camera, take and print pictures of your students acting out different vocabulary words and post them on a bulletin board. If one of the words you are focusing on that day is *surrounded,* you could take a picture of one student completely surrounded by other children, books, blocks, etc. You can also show children pictures that exemplify certain words and ask them what word the photograph represents.

Let Me Tell You About . . .

This activity gets the folks at home involved. Make copies of the "Let Me Tell You About . . ." reproducible on page 110 so there is one strip for each student. At the end of each day, take a few minutes to discuss with your students what they want their parents to ask them about when they get home. It might be a new vocabulary word, a story title, a concept, something that goes along with a science unit, anything at all. Whatever it is can be written on the strip. The point is to get adults and children talking. Parents can also write something on the strip for you to ask their child about the next day.

Let me tell you about . . .   What a butterfly eats
Let me tell you about . . .
Let me tell you about . . .
Let me tell you about . . .
Let me tell you about . . .

Would You Rather?

Ask your students questions using one or two oral vocabulary words you've already introduced. Based on your question, it's their job to make a choice. Once students get the hang of this, they may want to try asking questions of each other in small groups. If two of your words are *nibble* and *devour,* a question might be "Would you rather nibble on a candy bar or devour it?" The two words need not be related though. If your two words are *shabby* and *exquisite,* the question might be "Would you rather have a shabby backpack or an exquisite one?" You can also use this with just one word. If the word is *gnaw,* you might ask, "Would you rather gnaw on a shoe or a hot dog?"

Fill in the Blank

Provide students with sentence stems that require them to know the meaning of a word you've extracted from a story, and then ask them to complete your idea based on the word's meaning. For example: Arthur thought his sister was a nuisance because . . . (she was always bothering him), or Squirrels are always in a frenzy in the fall because . . . (they are getting ready for winter). For some basic vocabulary building, you can take this in a different direction and brainstorm words that would fit in a blank in a sentence. Anything will do here as long as there are many words that will make sense in a single blank. For example, you may say (or write): Yesterday afternoon I saw a dog _____. Or: There are a lot of fresh _____ at the grocery store. Children brainstorm ideas that would complete the sentence logically. You can choose to record their responses if you wish. If a child provides a response that does not make sense, be sure to explain why. For example, in the first blank above, if a child responded with *fly,* you might say, "Dogs can do many things but they cannot fly in real life. It would be cool if they could; dogs travel on the ground. Who can tell me something that does fly in the air?" It's important to explain why an answer does not make sense because it deepens children's understanding of words. Move the conversation back to the original sentence frame and continue as time allows.

Where Should Kids Be?

Assessment Checklist – 3 years

	Yes	No
Uses pronouns *I, you, me* correctly		
Understands a few spatial concepts such as *under*		
Knows main parts of the body or can indicate these if not name them		
Speaks easily in three-word sentences		
About 90% of what child says is intelligible		
Uses verbs that end in *-ing*		
Understands and answers most simple questions dealing with personal environment and activities		
Relates experiences so they are understood		
Begins to obey requests such as "put the block under the chair"		
Groups objects such as foods, clothes, etc.		
Identifies at least one color		
Uses most speech sounds		
Describes the use of objects such as *fork, car,* etc.		
Has fun with language. Enjoys poems and recognizes language absurdities such as, "Is that an elephant on your head?"		
Expresses ideas and feelings		
Repeats simple sentences		

Additional Notes

_____

_____

_____

Assessment Checklist – 4 years

	Yes	No
Knows names of familiar animals and names of common objects		
Knows more than one color		
Knows more than one shape		
Often indulges in make-believe		
Uses verbalization as he carries out activities		
Readily follows simple commands even if objects are not in sight		
Speaks in sentences of 4 to 5 words		
Uses past tense correctly most of the time		
Can speak of imaginary conditions such as "I hope"		
Asks many questions		
Understands some spatial concepts such as *behind* and *next to*		
Describes how to do things such as paint a picture		
Can list items that belong in a category such as *animals, vehicles*, etc.		
Can tell a simple story		

Additional Notes

_____

_____

_____

_____

Assessment Checklist – 5 years

	Yes	No
Knows common opposites		
Speaks intelligibly, even if he/she has articulation problems		
Defines common objects in terms of use (hat, shoe, chair)		
Knows his or her age		
Understands simple time concepts: morning, afternoon, night, day, later, after		
Uses some compound and some complex sentences		
Most speech is grammatically correct		
Understands time sequences (what happened first, second, third, etc.)		
Carries out a series of three directions		
Recognizes when words rhyme		
Engages in conversation		
Uses imagination to create stories		
Speaks in sentences of 5 to 6 words		
Knows most spatial relations like far and near		
Understands same and different		
Asks questions for information		

Additional Notes

_____

_____

_____

_____

Assessment Checklist – 6 years

	Yes	No
Uses many descriptive words spontaneously, both adjectives and adverbs		
Speech is completely intelligible and socially useful		
Tells a connected story about a picture		
Can tell what objects are made of		
Uses mostly compound and complex sentences		
Uses feeling words		

Additional Notes

Assessment Checklist – 7 to 8 years

	Yes	No
Handles opposite analogies: *girl-boy, man-woman, short-long,* etc.		
Understands terms such as *alike, different, beginning, end,* etc.		
Relates involved accounts of events that occurred at some time in the past		
Uses all kinds of sentences easily		
Has limited or no lapses in grammatical constructions, i.e., verb tense, pronouns, plurals		
Social amenities are present in speech in appropriate situations		
Control of rate, pitch, and volume are generally well established		
Carries on conversation close to adult level		
Follows multistep directions with little repetition		

Additional Notes

_____

_____

_____

_____

Home-School Connection

Dear Parent/Guardian,

There are so many wonderful things your child will learn this year! One area of development I'll be focusing on here at school each day is oral vocabulary. These are words your child uses correctly when speaking and understands when they are heard. Oral vocabulary also plays a big role in how well children understand what they read, and how much variety and interesting language they use in their writing. Parents often ask me what they can do at home to help their child succeed at school, so I'm including a list of simple activities that will help your child build a strong oral vocabulary.

- Talk about how objects are the same or different.

- Help your child tell stories using books and pictures.

- Let your child play with other children.

- Give your child your attention when he or she is talking.

- Talk about places you've been together or will be going to.

- Help your child sort things (food, stuffed animals, blocks) by color, size, shape, or any other characteristic.

- Teach your child how to use the telephone.

- Read long stories to your child.

- Let your child help you plan activities, such as what you will make for Thanksgiving dinner.

- Talk with your child about his or her interests.

- Let your child make up stories and tell them to you.

- Encourage your child to talk about feelings, thoughts, hopes, and fears.

- Sing songs and recite or read rhymes with your child.

- Talk with your child as you would with an adult.

- Look at family photos together and talk to your child about your family history.

You don't need to do all of these. Just keep them in mind as you and your child go about your normal routine and, most of all, have fun!

Sincerely,

CHAPTER 4

Strong Visual Systems: Paving the Road to School Success

In order to be good at something, we need to practice it over and over, and building our visual skills is no different. Our visual system is the foundation for just about everything we do. It allows us to do the obvious, like read the daily newspaper and see things in our path so we don't trip and fall. But that's really just the tip of the iceberg. As adults, our visual memory, processing, and discrimination allow us to remember what a colleague looks like, follow directions to a new restaurant, and enjoy our hobbies. Needless to say, it would be difficult to get along without them.

For children, however, this process of seeing is quite possibly the most crucial piece of their development. The strength of a child's visual "nuts and bolts" will affect them for the rest of their lives. In children, the visual processes revolve around recognizing the letters that will later combine to form words they need to read; forming letters and then placing them on the lines of paper; sorting, organizing, and remembering words and numbers; functioning in their environment; maintaining focus for the demands of school; and many other tasks.

The visual maturity of children entering school declines each year as more children spend more time in front of TV and computer screens and less time playing with puzzles, building and taking apart block structures, winding their way through paper-and-pencil mazes, doing word searches, finding hidden pictures, and playing outdoors with balls, buckets, and bicycles. The problem is becoming epidemic and will have serious consequences.

Visual skills develop over time, just like learning to walk or talk. They must become automatic just like walking and talking, too, but they can't without purposeful, consistent, long-term efforts from teachers, caregivers, and parents. The more automatically the visual system operates, the more learning takes place and with greater ease, so let's get going! Because many of the activities in this chapter will also contribute to children's gross and fine motor development (see Chapters 1 and 2), you'll really maximize their potential for school success.

What the Experts Say and Why It Matters

- Children with poorly developed visual skills will have to work harder throughout their school years to compensate for them.

- More visual activity than just the ability to see the letters is required in order for a child to read.

- Visual deficiencies may be a child's biggest hurdle to learning, but extraordinary gains in performance can be achieved by remediating the visual problem.

- Studies have linked vision dysfunction with juvenile delinquency. Vision problems make it difficult to achieve in school, leading to low self-esteem and disinterest in academics. Consequently, a child may develop negative behaviors that predispose him to delinquency.

- Besides reading, vision difficulties affect copying, spelling, and mathematics.

- Our visual systems also affect hand-eye coordination, athletic acumen, our ability to ride a bicycle, dance or move to a rhythm, and hear a sound (like a siren) and visually recognize where it's coming from without actually seeing the object.

- A poor visual system hinders the ability to give and get directions accurately.

- Visual deficiencies make it difficult for a child to learn left from right.

- Children who have underdeveloped visual skills are not able to cross the midline of their body easily, making efficient reading and writing nearly impossible.

- A poor sense of visual directionality may cause children to reverse letters when reading and writing, affecting their decoding, fluency, and comprehension.

- A child with an underdeveloped visual system will have trouble learning the alphabet, sight words, numbers, concepts of size and shape, and differences in color and orientation. She will also have difficulty discriminating between words that begin with the same letter.

- Difficulty concentrating, distractibility, and short attention span can result from visual inefficiencies.

Encouraging Development in This Area

Visual Perceptual Skill-Builders

Visual perceptual skills allow us to make sense of what we are seeing and to obtain and organize visual information from the environment. When we see two squares, even if they are different sizes, we know they are both squares because our visual perception tells us so. When children do puzzles, they are practicing discrimination skills as they take note of the distinct shapes and search through pieces, and figure ground (isolation) skills as they try to pick out the correct shapes from all the other ones. Any kind of shape-fitting or block-fitting task where kids have to place different-shaped pieces into the matching spaces or holes builds these skills as well.

Hidden pictures help a child develop the eye-teaming skills that keep him from seeing double. It's important, too, to use hidden pictures that provide the actual images of the objects being sought. This way the child knows exactly what form to find. Depending on his experiences, the child may picture a bird very differently from the one that is actually hidden in the picture.

Games that have been on the market for years and encourage visual perceptual growth include Battleship, Pictionary, Connect Four, and Perfection, to name a few. Most come in travel sizes that are great for lending out to families, and they fit very easily into backpacks!

Block Buddies

Make pattern cards by tracing pattern blocks into figures or abstract pictures. Children copy the pattern cards using the blocks to duplicate the pictures on the cards. Having to place the shapes oriented in the correct position helps the child learn about directionality and how flipping shapes affects the overall design. Tangrams, also an option, are best for slightly older children.

Marble Runs

Place a marble inside anything with sides, such as a box lid, dishpan, or cake pan. Have children manipulate the container to make the marble move around its perimeter. A variation on this is to place blank stickers in a random pattern on the bottom of a container. On each sticker write a number or letter in some sequence. Place a marble in the container and have students move the marble over the stickers by manipulating the container while saying the numbers or letters out loud. There are old-fashioned wooden block sets (such as Blocks and Marbles by Tedco) that children can place together in different configurations and let marbles run down the tracks. A traditional game of marbles works, too! No matter what you choose, the goal in any of these activities is to have children tracking (following) the marble with their eyes as it moves. But remember—children under three should not play with marbles.

Hidden Pictures Bingo

Give each student a copy of a hidden picture page, such as those you would find in a *Highlights for Children* magazine. Tell them that when you call out the name of an object, they are to search their pictures for the object. When a child finds it, he calls out "I see it!" Once verified and the location revealed, everyone finds and marks it on their sheets with a bingo chip or a highlighter. This continues until each object has been called out and found. A variation is to give children the same pictures or different ones, and the first to find all the objects is the winner. Another variation is for you and a child to work on the same picture together as a team and try to beat a timer.

Spotlight

Many children have difficulty with visual tracking, which makes reading and other academic tasks challenging. Play flashlight games with your students. These are fun, and children practice tracking skills without even knowing they are working. While sitting with your class in a darkened room, move the flashlight around and ask your students to follow the light with their eyes. If you wish, pause to talk about different objects the light stops at. Encourage older children to track the light with as little head movement as possible. Write letters or draw shapes with the light on a small area of a wall and have students try to guess the letter or shape. Then let the kids have turns with the flashlight.

Match Making

The game Memory is a tried-and-true favorite. It's easy to make customized versions, too, depending upon your needs. The visual piece here comes from the matching of letters, pictures, textures, shapes, numbers, or words. If you let students play in small groups, you are also encouraging valuable conversational skills. Besides physical matching games, children can build the visual perceptual skills they need by matching items on paper (drawing a line to connect the same items) or on notched cards (using yarn or rubber bands to indicate the matches). Matching objects to their drawn or dotted outlines is another easy option. Dominoes also require students to match images. You can use the dot configurations or make your own set that corresponds to a theme like farm animals or seasonal symbols. Students can play together or just match ends on their own.

By-Yourself-Bingo

Instead of playing in a whole group, this game can be played by a few children in a group or by an individual. Either way, each child gets a bingo board, a set of playing cards (or index cards with a number written on each one), and some markers. She draws a numbered card from the pile, compares it to what's on her board, and then marks her board if appropriate. Children playing in a small group can pass the numbered card to the next person or place it back in the pile so someone else can draw it. Children playing by themselves can actually place the numbered card from the pile on top of the corresponding box on their board.

Memory Trays

Place letters or numbers randomly on a tray or cookie sheet. Give students 10 seconds to study what's there and then have them close their eyes while you remove one letter or number. Then tell students to open their eyes and try to guess what you've removed. Be sure to show them the actual letter or number once it's been guessed to reinforce this for the others. If you really want to test their skills, just pretend to take something away every now and then. You can also turn this game around by adding something each time and asking students to identify the new letter or number on the tray. When doing this with younger children, use objects (penny, toy car, etc.) instead of letters or numbers.

Fun Font Sort

In order to be fluent readers, children need to be able to identify letters that are written in different ways. Choose several letters your students are already familiar with and print each in many different fonts on your computer. Use a large type size so they can be cut out and manipulated easily. Divide a piece of paper into a number of columns—one for each letter you made—and at the top of each column write a different letter in the way students are accustomed to seeing it. At a center, students can cut apart the letters in different fonts and paste them in the appropriate columns on their papers.

Visual Closure Cards

Visual closure is the ability to identify a form even though part of it is not visible. This allows us to glance at a word, maybe just noticing a few letters, and know what the word is by filling in the rest according to our visual memory of that word. To strengthen this skill, important for fluent reading among other things, show students half pictures or dotted outlines of familiar objects, shapes, letters, and numbers, and ask them to name what's pictured. Or provide portions of the picture or outline on laminated cards and have students complete the picture by drawing the rest of it on the card.

Visual Motor Skill-Builders

Visual motor skills refer to the ability to coordinate vision with the movements of the body. When we write our names, our visual motor skills allow us to make the strokes with our hand that will produce the visual picture of our name that exists in our head.

Visual motor skills are not usually developed in isolation but during daily gross and fine motor play and activities. In addition to the activities that follow, almost any of those you choose from Chapters 1 and 2 of this book will help build a child's visual system as well.

Flashlight Walking

Give a student two flashlights and ask her to hold one in each hand. With your classroom darkened, tell the student to walk in a regular manner and shine the opposing flashlight on the foot that is stepping forward. For example, she'll shine the flashlight in her left hand on her right foot as she moves that foot forward, and the flashlight in her right hand on her left foot as she moves it forward.

Copy Cat

In this game students copy the movements you initiate. For example, you can tap out rhythms on your arm or leg, or with your foot; make big shapes with your arms (like in the song "YMCA"); or march in place, raising each knee waist high. Students will track your movement and then put the visual motor part of their brains to work. Children can also take turns being the leader, if you desire.

Walk in My Shoes

Make a path of footprints on a piece of bulletin board paper, an old window shade, or anything else that you can get your hands on (well, your feet actually). Trace both left and right feet in walkable but random patterns. Once complete, have students walk the path, matching their feet to each foot on the paper. You can alter the orientation of a footprint to increase the level of skill required by the children to match their feet to the prints on the floor.

Keep Your Eyes on the Balloon

The full body movement required for balloon-tapping games is a terrific visual motor exercise. The students' goal is to keep the balloon in the air using arms, hands, feet, or any part of the body you specify. This can be done in a whole group or children can break up into smaller groups and work on their own. Add concept practice while they are doing this by asking students to recite sequences, like the months of the year, skip counting, or the alphabet.

Bats, Balls & Beanbags

Ball activities like throwing and catching, kicking, or using a "bat" (ping-pong paddle, empty soda bottle, soft bat) to hit a ball will all increase visual motor ability. It's important to remember to vary the size of the ball. Start with larger ones and decrease the size as students become more skilled. Children also enjoy bowling or knocking over blocks or other objects with a ball. Empty 2-liter soda bottles work well for this activity and if you allow children to set up the "pins" themselves each time, you are also developing other areas like wrist stability. Playing catch or target games by tossing a beanbag works well too.

Visual Arts

Art projects are so valuable here! They always involve motor planning and hand-eye coordination skills. Cutting fringe to create a lion's mane for a jungle unit or making a slithery snake for a unit on reptiles are examples of working art into the themes you already teach. Pass out the art supplies and help students build visual motor skills while having fun, too!

Trace & Track

Tracing activities such as mazes are terrific for building visual tracking skills. Keep them simple at first and then increase the level of difficulty as the child's ability develops. Your local dollar store is a good resource for pads full of mazes. Pictures made from tracing inside shape stencils are fun, too, and a good way to reinforce some math concepts.

Skill-Building Toys

There are lots of toys available commercially that promote visual motor skills, such as Etch-a-Sketch, Spirograph, Lite-Brite, Operation, and Pick-Up Sticks. Remember to check with friends, family, and colleagues to see if you can borrow any they are no longer using. Yard sales are also good places to find these toys.

Tactile Visual Cut-Ups

Let your students practice cutting in between pieces of yarn, popsicle sticks, sandpaper, and so forth, which provides tactile as well as visual input. Also have them cut out dot-to-dots (homemade, from the Internet, or from a workbook), which they can trace with their fingers first and then with writing utensils. Give them practice making letters, shapes, and numbers in various tactile media such as dry Kool-Aid, sand, cornmeal, salt, finger paint, on sandpaper or carpet squares, or with malleable items like Wikki Stix or pipe cleaners. You can also put ketchup, mustard, or shaving cream into a zip-top plastic bag, seal it securely, and let students make letters on the bag.

Assessment Checklist

Most of a child's general visual development happens by the age of four. Once children reach preschool age, the focus is on fine-tuning their skills. Much of that happens during fine motor development and as literacy skills increase. The checklist that follows describes behaviors that might be indicators of weaknesses or deficits in a child's visual system. I suggest conferring with parents, your school's occupational or physical therapist, the school nurse, and other experts in your building or district.

Appearance of Eyes and/or Complaints

	Yes	No
Red eyes or eyelids		
Excessive tearing		
Swollen or encrusted eyelids		
Frequent bumps or sores on lids		
Drooping eyelids		
Drifting of one eye when looking at an object		
Burning or itching eyes after doing desk work		
Headaches		
Eyes feel tired		
Print blurs after reading for a short time		
Nausea or dizziness		
Double vision		
Motion sickness		
Dislikes bright lights		

Additional Notes

_____

_____

_____

Behaviors

	Yes	No
Moves head instead of eyes when reading		
Loses place often when reading; needs finger or marker		
Tilts or turns head to see		
Squints; closes or covers one eye		
Has short attention span when doing desk work and/or reading		
Avoids reading		
Skips lines or words when reading		
Reads and rereads material to understand		
Writing slants up or down		
Has poor drawing orientation on a page		
Repeats letters within words when writing		
Confuses left-right directions repeatedly		
Poor hand-eye coordination		
Avoids detail activities like writing, coloring, or puzzles		
Bumps into objects, appears clumsy		
Holds materials being used unusually close		
Mistakes words with same beginning		
Fails to recognize same word in same or next sentence		
Whispers to self while reading silently		
Makes errors in copying near or far point (book to paper or board to paper)		
Mispronounces similar words		
Reverses letters or words beyond normal expectancy		
Transposes letters (*on* instead of *no*) or numbers (*12* instead of *21*)		

Additional Notes

_____

_____

Dear Parent/Guardian,

Did you know that 75 to 90 percent of all classroom learning takes place through a child's visual system? It's a surprising fact, and one that is not limited to how well your child sees. Clear vision is important, of course, but there are many other functions of your child's visual system that must be developed. Here are some simple suggestions for promoting your child's total visual development. (Tip: For games, puzzles, and books, check with family and friends to see if they have any you can have or borrow.)

* Play traditional games like Go Fish, Memory, or Slap Jack, and let your child be in charge of dealing or setting up the cards.

* Ask your child to copy shapes and lines that you make on a dry-erase board, in the mud, in a plate of salt, or in pudding or shaving cream spread evenly across a surface.

* Do arts and crafts projects with your child. Some simple seasonal activities are place mats with cutout shapes like leaves or hearts, old-fashioned paper chains that reflect seasonal or holiday colors, or greeting cards. If you need supplies, let me know.

* Let your child color. Print free coloring pages from the Internet or allow children to color the comics page from the daily newspaper. Make shapes on scrap paper and ask your child to color them in.

* Make two lines (wavy, straight, zigzag) with tape or sidewalk chalk and ask your child to drive a toy car between them.

* Encourage your child to complete puzzles. It's best to start with puzzles that contain only a few pieces and move up from there.

* Visit your local library and check out some of the I Spy books. Sit with your child and see who can find the most items on a page.

* Print mazes, word searches, tracing or matching pages, and finish-the-picture work sheets from the Internet. If you do not have a computer, try to do this at the local library, or visit a dollar store for inexpensive activity books that feature these.

No matter which activities you choose, they'll be more fun for your child if you do some of them together. It's a good way to share quality time and it's fun. Enjoy!

Sincerely,

CHAPTER 5

Language & Literacy: Getting Down to the Business of Letters and Words

Literacy instruction can and should begin long before children can actually read and write. I'm not talking about tutoring and torturing our preschoolers so they can read by the time they are three, but I *am* talking about setting the stage for literacy with rich, varied, and repeated experiences that revolve around language, letters, words, and books from the first moment possible. Among the most important aspects of early literacy development are alphabetic knowledge (recognizing letters, connecting the sound to the letter symbol), concepts about print (that we read from left to right, for example), phonological awareness (the ability to manipulate sounds orally), and rapid naming of objects and symbols.

In addition to language arts, work writing into other parts of the day There are opportunities to draw and write number stories during math, for example, or record observations of a bug during a science exploration. Think of these as double dipping. The more students write, the better writers they will be, and the more they see writing as a universal (across the curriculum) activity, the more likely they are to do it within a subject that is interesting to them.

You should write with them, too. Choose one day each week when you are writing while your students are. It can be a list of groceries or weekend errands, a quick note to a friend, some rhyming verses . . . whatever makes you happy as a writer. Every now and then, consider sharing some of your writing with your students.

A writing center is another way to get your students writing at different times of the day. There can be a different, specific task every week, or "children's choice"—students decide what to do. If you structure your whole-group writing time each day, I recommend letting children choose at a writing center. No matter how you decide your writing center should operate, be sure that some general supplies are always available: envelopes, adding machine tape, scrap paper, lists of classmates' names, graph paper, letter tiles, sentence strips, lined and unlined paper, a variety of things to write with, dry-erase boards and markers, spiral bound and composition notebooks, a picture collection, alphabet strips, self-sticking labels, and clipboards.

Because of your great teacher instincts, you do many things each day that help build your students' literacy, sometimes subconsciously. This chapter is designed to give you the impetus to do even more, to get parents involved, and to add to your literacy tool kit.

What the Experts Say and Why It Matters

- When provided with an environment rich in language and literacy and with opportunities to listen to and use language, 95 percent of children can acquire the essential building blocks for learning how to read and write.

- Knowledge of letters at kindergarten entry is predictive of reading ability in tenth grade.

- Almost all early literacy learning is based on literate behaviors modeled and supported by adults.

- A child who is a poor reader in first grade has a 90 percent chance of remaining a poor reader at the end of fourth grade.

- Children and adults do most of their learning through reading.

- The brain of a child in the age range two to six is twice as active as that of an adult and is primed for developing the foundations needed for the complicated processes of reading and writing.

- Solid literacy skills facilitate strong communication skills.

- Reading is the fundamental skill upon which all formal education depends.

- Once children begin formal schooling, classroom instruction, more than any other factor, is crucial to their reading and writing success.

- One of the best predictors of how well a child will function in school and go on to contribute actively to our society is the level of reading and writing attained by that child in her early years.

- The amount of exposure children have to the concepts of reading and writing before they can read and write themselves has more of an impact on their eventual independent reading and writing efforts than anything else.

- Children who are behind in reading ability in grade three are at risk of remaining behind in reading for the rest of their lives.

- Early literacy attempts such as "reading" pictures and scribble writing are the foundations of later literacy development and must be encouraged from the earliest time possible in a child's growth.

Encouraging Development in This Area

Reading All Around

One of the most important activities for building the knowledge required for success in literacy is reading quality literature aloud to children. Motivation is also an important factor; foster a love for the printed word and give a child a gift for life. If you have fun with words, children will too. So read aloud to them every day, and make literacy interactive and engaging. (See pages 113–114 for task cards to use with your children.)

Interactive Reading

Teach your students how to read interactively when you are sharing a story with them. Each time you say a sound word or use an exaggerated voice, ask students to repeat the word in the same way you read it. You may need to pause at first to cue them to use their voices, but they'll catch on quickly and become more active listeners. Active listening improves comprehension and expression!

Shared Reading

Shared reading uses big books or print in an enlarged format, such as in a pocket chart, a language experience chart, or on a transparency. Consider rhyming text—always popular with emergent readers. Choose books with simple, repetitive language and illustrations that closely match the text. One or two lines per page is best for emergent readers. On the first reading, you may choose to think out loud—teaching decoding, asking yourself a question, or making a connection to your reading. On subsequent readings, call your students' attention to initial consonants, punctuation marks, sight words, or anything else appropriate. Focus on just one skill each time you revisit the text. As children become familiar with it, allow them to read along chorally. Shared reading should be fast and light; keep it interesting and interactive.

Repeated Readings

Getting kids to reread is sometimes a struggle, so have them change positions each time they are rereading. They might read with their feet up on the table; sitting backward on their chairs; lying on the floor, propped up on their elbows or up on all fours; or sitting on the table with their feet on their chairs. Always model the safest way for them to get into and out of these positions.

Topic Tables

To increase literacy for a wide array of students, supply a table full of books, pictures, photos, maps, brochures, and items that relate to a specific topic, like the ocean. The reading materials should vary in difficulty, print size, and type of media. Provide nonreaders especially with pictures and unit-related objects to look at, handle, and discuss with others. Offering lots of different reading and browsing materials also helps you differentiate instruction; children can find what's just right for their readiness or interest level.

Sing It

Write the words (or just the chorus) to a song your children know on a piece of chart paper. After they've sung it for a few days, use the now-familiar text to teach letters, sounds, rhyming skills, sight words, and more. Remember, the best way to teach these skills is not in isolation but through meaningful print experiences.

Letter/Word Search

Using the blank grid on page 111, create a word search with a twist—the search will contain only one letter to look for now, and grow to include additional letters as students read more. Write the letter a number of times in the boxes of the grid and then fill in any remaining spaces with random letters. Also write the letter at the top of the grid. Each time the student finds the letter, he highlights it and writes it once in the letter bank. As students develop a sight word vocabulary, you can do the same activity with single words.

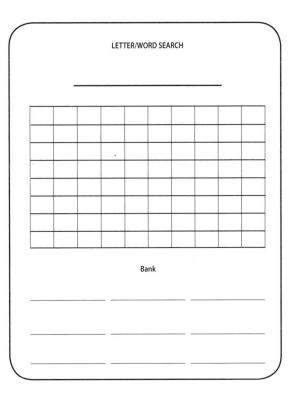

Stick to It

Write a poem on poster board or chart paper and display it in your rug area. Read it to your students, allowing them to participate as they are able. Then give a few children sticky notes and ask each one to cover a particular letter. After each child has placed her sticky note on the chart paper, take them down one at a time, read each letter as a group, and then together read the word that the letter appears in. Go back and read the sentence or line the letter was found in. Point out the same letter in another word and compare the placement of the letter to that of the earlier word, demonstrating that letters go in specific places in words, not just in random order.

Showing Off

Give students photocopies of an appropriate piece of text from your reading series, independent reading books, math lessons, or anything else students will have contact with. Read it to them once and then have them read it with you to the best of their ability. Once you've done several readings, ask them to use highlighting tape, highlighters, or yellow crayons to find a certain sound or sounds. For example, ask them to highlight all of the words that end with the /s/ sound. Check and correct as you go, being sure to enunciate the sound so it's heard clearly and pointing out its location for any student who missed it.

Alphabet Laundry

Tie a piece of clothesline between two table legs and put a container of clothespins next to the table. Laminate a supply of paper shapes that go along with the season or with weekly units or themes. Each week, choose a shape and write uppercase letters on some shapes and their lowercase mates on other shapes—one letter per shape. Children clip uppercase and lowercase matches to the clothesline and record what they clipped on a piece of paper that has outlines of the same shapes. You can use pictures here too. For example, students clip a picture of a ball and the letter *b* onto the clothesline.

Stamping Station

Supply students with rubber stamps and work sheets or cards that have letters written on them. Children find and stamp the correct letter next to each letter on the sheet or card. So if you used the lowercase letters *p, j, t,* and *d,* students would stamp a *p* next to the letter *p* on the card or work sheet, and so on. You can also write the uppercase version of letters and have students locate and stamp the lowercase version or vice versa. Similarly, you can provide pictures and have children stamp initial consonants or all the sounds they hear in a word. When students are ready, include consonant blends like *bl, sp,* and *tr.*

Food Carton Fun

Save clean, empty food containers (like cereal and cake mix boxes). Cut them apart, bring them to school, and invite children to find letters they know. Depending on the containers, you can laminate them, place them in plastic page protectors, or cover them with clear packing tape or contact paper for durability. At a center or during free time, students can scan the containers, circle any letters they know with a dry-erase marker, and share their findings with friends. This activity will also lead to lots of conversation about the foods described and children's likes and dislikes.

Stand Up, Sit Down

Program six or more large index cards with pictures that begin with the letters you want to focus on. Gather children into small groups and assign each group a different letter. Ask them to repeat for you what their letter is so everyone remembers. Hold up one card at a time. Let's say it has a picture of a word that begins with the letter *h*, such as *house*. The students who were assigned *h* stand up and sit down quickly. Continue with as many cards as you have time for, being sure to repeat each letter more than once so children stay focused.

Show Me

Give children five to ten blank index cards each. Ask them to write a different letter in uppercase and lowercase (you'll choose which ones) on each card and to lay the cards out in front of them. Make sure you have a set, too. Next, ask them to show you the letter *Kk,* for example. Each student holds up the card with that letter and makes the letter's sound. If a student's response is incorrect, hold up your card (in this case the *Kk* card) and say, "I should see a card like this. This is the letter *Kk*. It starts the word *kangaroo* and the name *Kyle*."

Relay Races

Program index cards with a few letters you are currently working on; make enough sets so each team will have one. Place the cards at one end of your race area. For this activity, divide children into relay teams. Call out a letter. The first child in each team runs, hops, shuffles, or skips (according to your direction) to the pile of cards, finds the letter, and brings it back to his team, moving in the same manner as before. Whoever gets back first with the right card wins that lap. Ask children to think of words that begin with the same letter and record them on the board. Repeat the race routine, using a new letter. This can be played with words, too.

Beach Party

Write letters on an inexpensive beach ball. Ask children to gather in a circle and then toss the ball to one of them. When she catches it, she reads the letter that's under her right thumb, and then tosses it to another child. Continue until everyone has had a turn (or two!). You can extend this activity by asking children to make the sound of the letter or say a word that begins with that letter. Or ask the whole group to sky-write the letter in the air. Do this with sight words when children are ready.

Hopscotch, Anyone?

Create traditional hopscotch outlines outside using chalk or inside on an old solid-colored carpet runner with paint. Each time you wish to play, write letters or words or tape index cards with letters or words on them in each box of the hopscotch outlines. Divide students into groups and allow them to play simultaneously. Traditional rules apply. Kindergartners may not be able to hop on one foot, so let them bunny hop, tiptoe, walk, or whatever is comfortable for them. As students move along to retrieve their beanbags, koosh balls, or whatever was thrown, ask them to read what's in each box out loud; group members can help each other. On the way back to the beginning, tell students it's a "free ride," so they don't have to read upside down.

Beanbag Toss

Draw and color several large rectangles of the same size onto sheets of poster board. Write a letter or word inside each rectangle. Arrange students in small groups and provide each group with a beanbag and a poster board that they lay on the floor. In turn, each member of the group tosses the beanbag onto a rectangle and identifies the letter or word it lands on. Group members may help each other. To take it one step further, give each child a checklist containing the letters or words on the poster board. As her beanbag lands on each rectangle and she identifies what's written, she checks it off her list.

From A to Z

On a large magnetic board that is within your students' reach, randomly arrange a set of magnetic letters on the upper half of the board. Leave the lower half of the board empty so there's room for students to place the letters in alphabetical order. To begin, a child finds the letter *A* and moves it to the lower half of the board. Then he tags a classmate and sits down. That child finds the letter *B*, places it after the *A*, and then tags a different student. Students continue in this manner until all of the letters of the alphabet have been moved to the lower section of the board and placed in alphabetical order. To conclude, have the class sing or recite the alphabet as you point to each letter. A variation is to randomly write letters of the alphabet on a chalkboard within students' reach. In turn, give each student the eraser and have her erase the letter that you describe. Give clues such as "I am the first letter of the alphabet. I am the first letter in the word *apple*. I make the sound /a/."

/b/, /b/, Bear!

This is an adaptation of Duck, Duck, Goose. Arrange your students in a circle and pick one child to be "It." Instead of saying "duck," the selected child chooses a letter or uses the letter of the week and says its sound as he touches each classmate's head.

When the child is ready to choose someone for the chase, he says a word that begins with the letter sound. Play continues until everyone has had a turn.

Sound-O

Use a commercial alphabet bingo game or make your own cards. Instead of calling out a letter for students to cover up, call out its sound. The first child to complete a row shouts, "Sound-O!"

Sound Smack

Place a few letter, blend, digraph or word cards in front of each student. Give them something to smack the cards with, like a small flyswatter (their hand will also do). Pose random questions about the cards, which students respond to by smacking a particular one. If the letters being used were *f, t,* and *b,* you might ask, "Which letter says /b/?" (students would smack the *b*); "Which letter begins the word *top*?" (students would smack the *t*), and so on.

Syllable or Sound Whacker

Ask students to tap their arm or leg once with their hand or small flyswatter for each syllable (or sound) they hear in a word you say. Model and correct as necessary. If sounds are the focus, they can "sweep" the sounds together by running their opposite hand down the arm where they tapped the sounds out initially. So if the word was *pat,* a child would tap out /p/, /a/, /t/ and then sweep the sounds together to say the word *pat.* Use vocabulary, spelling, or sight words that students will come across in print in the weeks to come.

Plus & Minus

Using plastic cubes or bingo chips, ask students to show you the number of phonemes (sounds) in a word you say. If the word was *matter,* there would be four: /m/, /a/, /t/, /r/. After students have laid out the correct number of objects, ask them to take the first one away, which would be the /m/ sound. So students would be left with the phonemes /a/, /t/, /r/. Then ask students what word they would have if they added /b/ to the sounds they already have (*batter*), and so on. The words can be simple or more complex according to students' needs. After they've done this with a word, have students make an attempt at writing it, or have them tell you how they think it should be spelled while you record it on the board.

Carpet Square Affair

Acquire carpet squares from a local merchant or borrow some from a colleague. On each square make a letter or blend with duct or masking tape, and then place them on your rug area in a circle. Be sure that each letter or blend can combine with a rime to make a word. When children come to the rug for group time, assign each one to a particular place by stating the letter or blend shown there. As children go to their places, ask them what word their square would make if combined with -at, for example. So if you asked a child to find and sit on the blend /fl/, they would locate it and say *flat*.

Picture This

Use picture cards of any sort and ask students to listen for a target sound (which you will designate) as you name the pictures. Their job is to tell you where they heard the sound. For example, if the target sound is /g/ and the picture shows a pig, the students should say the target sound is at the end. Depending on the ages and readiness levels of your students, use pictures of everyday items, or ones that relate to a current unit of study.

Name Game

Gather a large number of things you can write individual letters on, like poker chips, milk lids, small ceramic tiles, or bingo chips. Use a permanent marker to write the letters of each child's name (including the uppercase letter at the beginning) on separate chips or lids and put each set of name chips in a zip-top plastic bag with the child's name written on it in permanent marker. Give students their bags of letters, and have them work in small groups. They mix up their letters with those of their partners or group members, and arrange them in one big pile in the middle of their group, making sure all the letters are face down. In turn, each child turns over only one lid or chip to reveal its letter. The group names the letter and makes its sound together. If the letter is in the child's name, he keeps it; if not, he turns it back over, and the next child has a turn. The first child to spell his name correctly (including the uppercase letter at the beginning) is the winner.

Word Family Fun

Create a series of empty boxes on a piece of paper. Write a word from the same family in each box (*cake, bake, rake*) and make a copy for each student. Ask children to draw a picture to represent each word. You can also leave a blank space at the beginning of each word (*_ake*) and ask students to fill in a letter to create a word and then draw it.

Writing Opportunities Abound

To become good writers, students need to write every day, even before they really know how. Most of us would not dream of skipping reading instruction, and we need to bring that same dedication to our writing instruction. Children will not learn to write without numerous, varied opportunities to experiment with writing tools and reasons to write. It's nonnegotiable.

Make-a-Word

Give each student letter and word tiles (make or purchase them), a laminated sentence strip, and a dry-erase marker. Each child chooses a word tile and places it on her strip. Then she makes the same word with letter tiles and places them on the strip next to the word. Finally, she writes the word on the sentence strip with the marker. After making and reading the word three times, she erases the word on her strip and disassembles the letter tiles, which she'll use again to make another word.

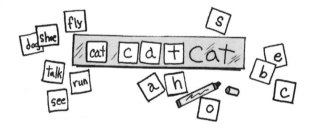

I've Got a Story

Students always have a story they want to share with you so ask them to record their stories on paper during a writing session or free time. Some common themes might be: How I Lost a Tooth, Stories of Our Cuts and Bruises, or An Amazing Thing Happened. Even if your students are not yet writing in the traditional sense, this conveys the idea that something that happened to them is worth writing down.

Big Word of the Week

Each week, scramble the letters in a "big" word that's related to your current unit of study. Using the reproducible grid on page 112, write the letters across the top. Children make as many small words as they can using the letters in the big word, and record them in the boxes. Practice this a few times as a group, using children's names, before you ask them to do it on their own. In the beginning of the year, they may be filling only a box or two with simple words like *I, a, it,* and so on. As time goes by and as children develop at their own rates, they will make more. To scaffold this activity, provide students with letter tiles to manipulate as they attempt to make new words.

Big Word of the Week

Name __Lisa__

Use the scrambled letters below to make as many words as you can. Do you know what word these letters make?

a i h t a b

a	hat	it	bat	at

Journals

There are many opportunities for journal writing. Children can have daily writing journals, science observation journals, reading response journals, weekend journals, and personal journals. For younger writers you'll want to use blank pages or half-lined/half-blank pages. For older students you can alternate blank and lined. Be sure to check in with a few students each day and ask them what they wrote. You may wish to record what they tell you if it's not clear. Remember, early literacy is about getting strokes, letters, and strings of letters onto paper. Be careful not to bog down young writers with too many conventions and expectations—at least for now.

Writing Grab Bag

Keep your writing routine interesting to motivate students. While journal writing has its benefits, it will get boring fast if you ask students to do it every day. So once a week, get out your writing grab bag. Copy, laminate, and cut apart the task cards reproducibles on pages 117–122. Make sure there are enough for all your students, plus a few extras, and put them in a bag—your writing grab bag. At writing time, pull out the bag and let each student select a card from it and complete the writing task on the card.

Drawing to Write

Give students ten minutes to sketch whatever they are going to write about (in this example, a favorite spot or place). When time is up (they do not need to finish their drawing), divide them into small groups and have each child tell the rest of the group about the place in his picture. The other children in the group should ask questions about things they want more information on (like the trophy Gina drew on her bedroom dresser). Once each child has asked a question, another group member explains his picture and the process is repeated until everyone in the group has shared his picture and answered questions about it. Have children go back and "write" more about their pictures, and remind them to include some of the information their classmates wanted to know. Then give them a few more minutes after they've written to add more details to their sketches.

Interactive Writing

Besides letting children write on their own, write with them —"sharing the pen," so to speak. Interactive writing is my favorite way to do this. You can teach everything in your state's writing standards and be a good model at the same time. Many teachers have their own versions of this, which is fine, but there are a few universal points to remember:

- Keep the writing session brief and focused; a piece of interactive writing doesn't need to be completed in one sitting.

- Even if you're writing on the big board, give every child a small board to write on during the lesson, or you'll lose them for sure (trust me!).

- Relate the writing to something you've done together or something your children are familiar with—good writers write about what they know.

- After every addition to the piece (even if it's just one word), read the whole thing together.

- Share the pen—literally; a child might write the initial consonant or blend of a word you're going to use and you supply the irregular rime.

Have It Your Way

Each week make a wavy line, a zigzag, a large dot, or any kind of mark or series of marks on the reproducible on page 123 and make a copy for every child. Ask students to create a pencil drawing that incorporates the mark you made, and then write something about it on the picture (labeling) or on the lines below.

It's in the Bag

Give each student a grocery bag that has the letter her name begins with written on it (large and dark). Also provide either pictures of objects one would find in a grocery store, or the objects themselves, that begin with a variety of letters. Each student then either fills her bag with objects that begin the way her name does or glues pictures of those objects to the outside of her bag. When students are finished, allow each one to show off her bag and the items she selected. Each time an object is pointed out, the rest of the students practice making the letter sound or writing the letter on small dry-erase boards you have provided. If there's time, ask students to "write" a grocery list based on what they put in their bags. Standard spelling is not the goal here; it's giving children opportunities to write for authentic reasons.

How to Get Literacy Builders into the Home

1. Create reading and writing kits that a few children take home each night. A reading kit might contain wordless picture books, easy readers, a book about a current unit of study, or a class-made book. A writer's kit might have different kinds of paper (lined and unlined), a selection of writing utensils, a clipboard, a list of classmates' names, a list of common word families and their members (*it, sit, bit, hit, lit,* etc.), and a collection of pictures. You don't need any assignments to go along with these take-home kits—the goal is simply to get materials that encourage literacy efforts into the hands of families that may not have them.

2. If you write a morning message on chart paper, send it home with a different student each day to practice reading with someone there.

3. At conference time, ask a volunteer to sit outside your classroom with library card applications from your local library. While parents are waiting to speak with you, the volunteer can help them fill out the forms (if necessary), take them to the library the next day, and drop off the cards at school so you can send them home.

4. Share "Tips for Reading with Your Child" (see pages 114-115) in your weekly or monthly newsletter. Send home one tip or the whole sheet. Each week add others to your newsletters, and invite parents to send you tips they've discovered. Share these in your newsletters. The Reading Is Fundamental website (www.rif.org) is a good resource, too.

5. Besides lending books to families who may not have them, consider making books-on-tape available (and the equipment to play them as well) for families where the adults cannot afford to rent or buy them or have poor literacy skills or a primary language other than English. Ask parents or grandparents who want to volunteer but can't get into the classroom to record books for you. Team up with a 4th or 5th grade teacher and have her fluent readers record for you. You can also contact your state's association for the blind as some will provide this service free of charge.

6. Record alphabet or rhyming songs with your children at school and let them take the tapes and tape player home so they can sing with their families. Rhymes, repetition, and patterns help build children's phonemic awareness.

7. Place several pictures or small objects inside a clean sock. Send the sock home with a different student as often as you wish. Tuck a note inside that reads, "This is a story sock. Help your child make up a story about some or all of the items inside. If you want, you can write your child's story down and add it to the sock before you send it back to school. Either way, have fun!" You may want to model this activity and create a few stories with your students before you start sending the sock home so they can "instruct" their parents on how it's supposed to go.

Where Should Kids Be?

Assessment Checklist – 3 to 4 years

	Yes	No
Enjoys listening to and discussing storybooks		
Understands that print has a message		
Engages in reading attempts such as "reading" pictures		
Engages in writing attempts such as scribbling		
Identifies familiar labels and signs in environment		
Participates in rhyming games		
Identifies some letters		
Makes some letter/sound matches		
Uses known letters and "close enough" letters to represent messages		

Additional Notes

_____

_____

_____

_____

Assessment Checklist - 5 years

	Yes	No
Enjoys being read to		
Retells simple stories or information from text read to him		
Sounds as if she is reading when she pretends to read		
Uses descriptive language to explain events, people, and places		
Recognizes letters		
Recognizes letter/sound matches		
Shows familiarity with rhyming sounds		
Shows knowledge of beginning sounds		
Understands concepts of print (left to right, top to bottom)		
Matches spoken words with written ones		
Begins to write letters of the alphabet		
Begins to write high-frequency words		

Additional Notes

_____

_____

_____

_____

Assessment Checklist - 6 years

	Yes	No
Reads familiar stories		
Retells familiar stories		
Uses reading strategies such as rereading and context clues for comprehension		
Initiates independent reading		
Initiates independent writing activities		
Reads orally with some fluency		
Uses word parts and letter sounds to decode new words		
Identifies an increasing number of high-frequency words		
Represents most pronounced sounds when spelling words		
Writes about topics meaningful to him		
Attempts to use punctuation and capitalization		

Additional Notes

_____

_____

_____

_____

Assessment Checklist – 7 years

	Yes	No
Reads with reasonable fluency		
Uses more reading strategies efficiently to improve comprehension		
Uses effective word identification strategies		
Identifies an increasing number of high-frequency words		
Writes for a variety of reasons and audiences		
Uses common word-family patterns to achieve conventional spelling		
Uses correct punctuation on simple sentences		
Proofreads own work		
Reads daily		
Reads for information		

Additional Notes

Assessment Checklist – 8 years

	Yes	No
Reads fluently		
Uses a wide range of strategies to improve comprehension		
Uses word identification strategies automatically		
Makes connections between texts		
Recognizes and discusses different text elements		
Writes in many genres (poetry, stories, reports . . .)		
Has/uses a rich vocabulary appropriate to situation		
Revises and edits own work		
Uses conventional spelling		

Additional Notes

_____

_____

_____

_____

Home-School Connection

Dear Parent/Guardian,

You are your child's first and most important teacher. This is especially true when it comes to literacy skills—that is, what a child knows about reading and writing, even before he or she is able to read and write independently. Your child's literacy skills benefit greatly when adults are involved with and responsive to his or her attempts to use, read, and write language.

What you do now to encourage literacy at home will make a difference in the rest of your child's life. Below is a list of simple activities that will help your child build these skills.

- Let your child see you reading and writing each day. Talk with your child about what you are reading and writing. You might say, "I'm not sure how to spell this word. I'll say it slowly and listen for the sounds I hear," or, "I'm asking Dad a question in this note, so I'd better use a question mark."

- Read to your child every day; children may borrow books from our classroom library anytime. Share wordless books or just talk together about the pictures you see in books, magazines, or newspapers.

- Place alphabet magnets on your refrigerator or on a metal cookie sheet. When you are working in the kitchen, ask your child to name the letters and the sounds they make, and invite him or her to try to spell some words. Don't worry if a word is not spelled exactly right! Learners are concentrating on sounds they hear, especially at the beginning and end of a word.

- Set up a space or fill a tote bag with writing materials, such as scrap paper, envelopes from junk mail, pens, pencils, crayons or markers. Then your child will have a place to write and the materials to write with whenever he or she is ready.

- Buy alphabet soups and cereals and practice finding "letters of the day" with your child as you eat.

- Outdoors, play "I Spy." Look around and say, "I spy something that starts with the /m/ sound. What is it?" If you like, add clues, such as, "It's where we put and receive letters and bills."

- At the beach or in the mud, try making giant-sized letters by walking their shapes. Pretend you are writing messages to airplanes that might pass overhead.

- Point out printed words in the places you take your child, such as the grocery store, as well as individual letters on signs, billboards, posters, food containers, books, and magazines. Ask if he or she knows what sound the letter makes.

- Keep a small metal tray and set of magnetic letters in your car or in the bag you bring on the bus or subway. Let your child sort and match the letters, and copy short words he or she sees along the way.

- Bring along a flyer, brochure, or page from an old magazine when you and your child go to the doctor's office or the bank. Circle one letter on the page and invite your child to find and circle matching letters.

- Visit the local library—it's free!

As always, choose the activities that work best for you and your routines, and have fun!

Sincerely,

CHAPTER 6

Mathematics Makes the World Go 'Round

Even in the earliest years of their lives, children notice and explore math in their environment. Toddlers know (and let us know too!) when we have more cookies than they do or when a sibling's slice of pizza is larger than their own, even if they cannot put words to it. Preschoolers know the basic sequence of their daily schedule and can state comparisons at the grocery store about size or number.

Adults who have had negative experiences with math as students think of it as a subject to be avoided. If you fall into this category, put those memories aside. You have the opportunity to build on young children's exploratory and adventurous natures. Make time to talk about math, ask them about math, read to them about math, and help them discover all the math around them. When we use the word *math,* we're talking about more than "What's 2+2?" and "How many?" We're also considering questions such as "Will it fit?" "Is it likely to happen?" "How big is it?" "What comes next?"

Math is a part of everything we do every day. We just need to show students how and then capitalize on their inquisitive natures. In the beginning, you'll make the connections for your students: "Look, those shapes on your socks go all the way around your ankle, over and over again. See? It's a pattern. What shapes would we need to keep the pattern going all the way up your leg?" Soon they'll be initiating the connections: "Mrs. Reynolds, did you know that if you took my cracker and turned it a little, it makes another shape?"

Mathematical conversations can happen at snack time, recess, writing time, and throughout your day, so be on the lookout for opportunities to bring mathematical ideas to light and to life all day, every day.

Besides solid strategies and engaging activities, we also need to think about how we approach math in general with children. Manipulating math and talking about math are two highly underutilized techniques that the research says are crucial. What does that mean for math instruction? It means not only listening to Billy when he says that his dog is doing math but also asking Billy what he means. Instead of just dismissing it as a childish notion, take advantage of the opportunity. You might be surprised when this five year old tells you that his dog is the same on both sides (symmetry) and that when his dog had puppies, she did addition. If they can't put mathematical words to their observations, we need to give them the language from the very start. We need to teach mathematics differently from how we were taught. The best way for young children to learn these skills is to build conceptual understanding by interacting mathematically with their world and talking math. Remember, math is more than memorizing.

What the Experts Say and Why It Matters

- Mathematics is a pillar of formal schooling and its development is recognized as part of a child's well-being.

- When children enter kindergarten with a good grasp of fundamental mathematical concepts, they do far better in school endeavors.

- Positive early math experiences have positive long-lasting outcomes.

- When a greater emphasis is placed on early mathematics, children are prepared not only for future academic success but also for future career requirements.

- Encouraging early, multiple math strategies will make math accessible to more children because their natural learning styles will be targeted more often.

- The more time students spend early on experiencing math in different ways and building concepts, the deeper their understanding will be. With a strong foundation in place, they will learn more advanced math concepts with greater ease.

- Children who develop mathematical skills early have a stronger sense of their own abilities to figure things out.

- It is difficult to learn complex mathematical content without first having the foundations, and it is nearly impossible to build these skill areas simultaneously as demands in school become greater.

- Few if any differences in young children's abilities to learn mathematics are linked to gender or socioeconomic status; it's the teaching that makes the difference.

- When mathematics is taught properly at the early childhood and elementary levels, all children can develop proficiency in it.

Encouraging Development in This Area

First Things First

We need to talk about math with children as much as possible. Have a list of math questions posted someplace where you will see it often, and send the same list home to parents. There's nothing magic about the list; it's just remembering to use it. Once you pose a question, the talk about math comes easily and naturally. It's just a conversation. Here are some examples of the kinds of questions that can stimulate mathematical thinking and extend conversations: How are these alike? How are these different? What's another example of that? How do you know that's true? How would you convince me? What might be true . . .? What if . . .? What patterns do you see? What is always true about . . .? What is this all about? What "parts" does this have? Which is quicker/clearer/easier/ . . .? Which do you prefer? Why?

Also consider including a math center or two each week in your centers rotation and creating a set of "math choice" shelves with puzzles, blocks, nesting toys, pattern blocks, math songs on tape, simple math books, counters, file-folder games, dice, counting games like Candyland or Chutes and Ladders, hidden pictures (of numbers, shapes, or patterns), interlocking blocks, tiles, measuring tools, and anything else you can round up. While our interaction with children who are learning to think mathematically is crucial, it's also important for them to have time to explore on their own or to talk with a classmate about a mathematical discovery they just made. There's no such thing as too much practice with mathematical thinking, so consider opportunities to use math in art, language arts, science, and social studies lessons.

Pre-Counting Skills

This set of skills involves pairing and one-to-one matching (a shoe with a sock, a pencil with an eraser, etc.), sorting by any characteristic, classifying (things we eat and things we do not), rote counting or reciting number words in sequence, one-to-one correspondence (orally labeling each object with a number, even if the numbers are not correct), and seriation, or arranging objects in a position or series or by size.

One-to-One

Do one-to-one matching activities with young children to help them develop conservation of number. Here's one example: use a pile of something large, like socks for adults, and a pile of something small, like socks for infants, with the same number of objects in each pile. The child will remove one infant sock and you will remove one adult sock. Repeat the process so that the child can see that the number of socks is the same even though one group of socks is much bigger. It doesn't matter what you use in this activity; the point to make is that different-sized items grouped together can contain the same number or quantity, and that if we take from or add to one group, it becomes smaller or bigger in the process. If they are simply rearranged, the number stays the same. These concrete experiences need to be repeated often to enable a child to manipulate the items and become engaged in the process.

Line Up

Provide individuals or groups of students with a collection of three different-sized blocks, shoes, coins, cans, buttons, or whatever you have. Then ask them to place the items in order by size: large, larger, largest, or small, smaller, smallest. Increase the number of objects as children become more skilled, making sure that the objects all differ in size.

Sticker Stumper

Use stickers to make patterns on a page or classify them by attributes. Arrange a row of a set number of stickers, and then arrange a second row with the same number of stickers, but with more space between each one. Ask students if both rows have the same number of stickers or if one row has more stickers or fewer stickers. Ask how they can find out without counting (match the stickers one to one).

Look Away

Arrange common classroom items (eraser, block, crayon, etc.) on a tray and show them to the child. Then ask her to look away while you rearrange the items, and show them to her again. Ask her if the number of items is still the same or if it's different.

Count Out Loud

Playing oral counting games whenever possible equips kids with important pre-math skills. Ask them to count the number of blocks in a basket, fingers you hold up, items in a picture (*I Spy* books are great for this), steps in the hallway, sections on a lunch tray, buttons on a shirt, or anything else. The key is to do it often and in a variety of contexts so children see that no matter what we are counting, the pattern is always the same. Counting by different intervals (2s, 3s, 5s, 10s . . .) and counting backward also need to be included, as should counting from random numbers (for example, start at 12 and count to 31).

Sing a Song

Sing number rhymes and songs (we're not worried about them reading here), like "Five Little Monkeys," "One Potato, Two Potato," and "This Old Man." A good resource for seasonal counting songs is *Mailbox* magazine. Check also with your music teacher and colleagues; you'll have more counting rhymes and songs than you'll know what to do with!

Match Play

Provide students with zip-top plastic bags containing two different kinds of objects, but the same number of each (15 blocks and 15 pennies, for example). Ask students to match one block to each penny. If your students are developmentally ready, do this as a cut-and-paste activity. Provide them with a sheet of squares and triangles. Ask them to cut out all of the shapes, and then have them glue them together on a blank sheet of paper in one-to-one correspondence, one square to one triangle.

Partner Pull

Place a handful of small blocks, Unifix cubes, or buttons in between a pair of students and give each one a small plastic cup. For

each round of play, one child at a time places her cup upside down onto the pile and drags the cup toward her. Once both players have done this, they count the objects they were able to pull from the pile with their cups. Students compare numbers, using a hundred chart if necessary, and determine which number is larger. Both players return the items to the pile and start again.

Rollin', Rollin', Rollin'

Give each student a laminated number grid, a die, and a dry-erase marker. Divide students into pairs or small groups. In turn, each student rolls the die and colors that many spaces on her grid. The first child to get to 100 (or 25 or 50) wins that round and play can start again if time allows. You can also use a blank grid with no numbers.

Top Secret Sort

Divide children into groups of two or three. Give each group a handful of buttons, beads, and other small items of different shapes and sizes. One person in the group will sort the items into two or three piles without revealing his top-secret categories. When he has finished, the other students in the group need to figure out how the objects were sorted. When the first student's categories have been revealed, the next student in the group takes a turn and sorts the objects using different criteria. Students can do this independently as well, and then have a conversation with an adult about the sorting criteria they used.

Developing Number Sense and Counting Skills

This group of skills revolves around how numbers relate to each other, what patterns they hold, what numbers and sets look like, and the actual act of counting—knowing that "2" means there are two of something.

Round Off!

Supply each student with a laminated blank, grid-style game card, game markers like pennies or bingo chips, and a dry-erase marker. Ask students to write the numbers 10, 20, 30, 40, 50, 60, 70, 80, and 90 in the boxes of the game card, repeating any of the numbers they choose until they fill all of the boxes. Call out a number (74, for example). Ask students to determine which 10 the number 74 would be rounded off to and to mark that number on their game card (in this case, it would be 70). After students have marked their cards, state the correct answer and show why on a number line. Continue calling numbers until someone fills in an entire row and calls "Round Off!"

ROUND OFF!

70	40	10	30
60	90	50	80
10	20	40	60
30	70	80	20

The Puzzler

You can use a traditional hundred chart for this or create your own to reflect number sequences your students are working on. Simply duplicate the grid onto sturdy paper, laminate, and cut each one apart into the number of pieces desired. Store the pieces in zip-top plastic bags for students to use when they've got a few minutes on their hands. They can work together, race each other, or complete the puzzles independently.

Beach Ball Counting

Write numbers on an inexpensive beach ball. Toss it to one student. As each child catches it, she must read the number that her right thumb lands on and then toss it to the next person. Continue until everyone has had a turn (or two!). If you wish to add additional skills at another time, ask students to read the number and tell you what number is one more or one less or ten more or ten less. Students can also be asked to create an addition fact that equals the number their thumb landed on, a subtraction fact, or another way to represent that number if they are ready.

Partner Place Value

Pair up students and give each individual either two or three number dice, depending on what place value you wish to focus on. Students roll their dice simultaneously, and each child makes the largest number she can with the numbers she's rolled. Together each pair reads their two numbers out loud and determines whose number is larger. Then they gather up the dice and both roll again, this time trying to make the smallest numbers they can. If students need concrete representation to make number comparisons easier, allow them to use base ten blocks or something similar to build their numbers.

Keep Your Calendar

Because of time constraints, many educators have set aside calendar time. If you're in that category, it's time to rethink your decision. A daily, extended calendar time (15 minutes or so) is one of the best ways to review and reinforce many math concepts in a short period of time and let each child contribute at her level of readiness. Here you can review ordinal numbers, other names and representations for numbers, greater than, less than, equal to, place value, computation, shape and number patterns, seriation, and more.

Computation

Computation skills involve more than just memorizing addition or subtraction facts. Although mental math skills are important, memorizing without knowing why and how the parts make the whole will not help our children move beyond the lowest level of mathematical thinking: recall. Computation and understanding are developed first through the manipulation of props and pictures (concrete representations), and then without (using numbers and symbols); next, by simple trading (three small beans for one big bean); then through the construction and deconstruction of sets (add one to each row or take one away); and finally, by analyzing and solving word problems. There are many engaging, interactive ways to practice these skills, so remember to move beyond the drill-and-kill style of teaching computation.

Problem of the Day

As part of their morning work, ask students to answer the problem of the day. Write a word problem on the board and have children respond in a journal or on a piece of paper. If students are not reading yet, begin each math period by sharing a word problem orally and allowing children to work out the solution with manipulatives.

Fact-o-File

Laminate a number of file folders. On the outside of each one, write a different number that you want your students to create math facts for. (Write only one number on the outside of each folder and make sure each one is different.) Give each student a folder and a dry-erase marker. If students are still at the concrete stage, place the file folder and marker in a zip-top plastic bag, along with the appropriate number of manipulatives. It's each student's job to write addition or subtraction facts on the inside of her folder that equal the number on the outside. Students may check each other, check with you, or use a calculator to check themselves—it's okay! Next, ask them to erase the inside of their folders and trade with a peer for additional practice.

Toss & Total!

Give each student a copy of the game card reproducible on page 124, a dry-erase marker, and a pair of dice. Explain that each student will toss her dice, add up the numbers, and color in the box on the card that corresponds to her sum. Stop the game after five minutes and ask each student to identify which sum occurred most often on her card.

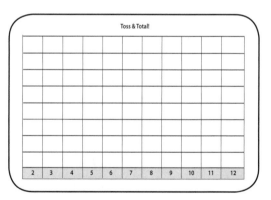

Picture the Problem

Write some simple addition and/or subtraction word problems and share them with your students. Allow each student to select one problem and draw a simple representation of it on a dry-erase board with a dry-erase marker. Once students have become comfortable with this, allow each one to draw a picture first, and then write or share with the group a word problem that matches with the picture he has drawn.

Herding Children

Getting children physically involved in math is one of the best ways to make it stick, so try this. Ask students to stand in one big group in the middle of your rug. In a fun yet gentle manner, herd a few children to one side of the rug and a few to the other side, leaving some in the middle. Count those in the side groups and ask students to create an addition and a subtraction sentence out of the two numbers. So if you herded 7 children to one side and 3 to the other, their answers would be 7+3=10 and 7−3=4. Help with the calculations as needed. If you want to take their thinking further, move a child from one side group to the other, or move a child from the middle to one of the groups and repeat the questioning process. Remember, it isn't enough for them just to know the answers; we need to help them make the connections by talking mathematically: "We added one child, so to find out how many we have now, all we have to do is add one to the sum we just had—we don't need to count all over again." Do this repeatedly to make sure that all children have a chance to be "herded" from the middle group.

Geometry

Geometry involves the ability to recognize similarities and differences among shapes and to match, find, combine, construct, describe, talk about, and alter shapes (varying size and orientation). Children develop an awareness of shapes when they engage in stacking them, lining them up, creating pictures with them, and classifying them. Children need rich, varied, and repeated exposure to the names of shapes and their attributes, and they need ample opportunities to play with shapes. Through their play, they will make patterning and sequencing discoveries. Play is children's work; keep in mind that playing with shapes is not only for our youngest learners. Older children will simply make more complicated, advanced connections.

Shape & Tape

Supply each student with highlighting tape or Wikki Stix and a magazine, catalog, or book. Ask students to look through the media you have provided for complex shapes or for shapes that fit specific criteria. Once they've found the appropriate shapes, they isolate them with their tape or Wikkis.

Parts & Pieces

Before class, draw a variety of shapes on a piece of tagboard and laminate it. Make one for each student you are working with. Along with the tagboard, give each student eight 2-inch strips of highlighting tape. Ask them to use the tape to mark the parts of a shape you specify. You might have them mark all the sides of a shape, all the corners, or (if you've included 3-D shapes) all the flat or curved faces. On another day, repeat the process but substitute 3-D blocks for the tagboard.

4 Corners Geometry

Cut pictures from magazines, catalogs, or other resources that reflect shapes you wish to focus on. You'll need enough so that each child can have one. Prepare four index cards, each with the name and outline of a shape. Give the cards to four different students and ask them to go to the four corners of your rug or your room. Distribute the pictures you have cut out to everyone else, one picture per child. When everyone has a picture, ask them to sort themselves into the four corners according to the shape that is represented in their pictures. So if a child has a picture of a pizza, she would find the person in a corner who has the index card for the circle and stand in his corner. Students can and should help each other, so give them a few minutes to do this on their own, assisting only if necessary.

Partner Shape Up

Laminate one index card for every two students. Use Wikki Stix to create a shape on each card, and then cut each one into two pieces, leaving the Wikki Stix in place. Give each child one piece of an index card. Explain that on your signal, the students will mingle with their peers until each one finds the person who has the other half of his shape. The pair can sit together until all shapes have been reunited. Then allow each pair a moment to stand up and share their shape and its name. Redistribute the cards and repeat the process.

Shape Sort

At a center, place a box of pictures cut from magazines (of a beach ball, a pyramid, or a TV screen, for example) and a set of large index cards, each labeled with a shape name represented by the pictures. (For nonreaders, for scaffolding, or for young kids, you might want to have a drawing of the shape as well as the shape name on the cards.) Children visiting this center sort the pictures onto the appropriate index cards. You can also ask students to make patterns with the shapes. As students become more skilled, use complex shapes like trapezoids and cylinders. A great math-to-world connection!

Mix It Up

Be sure to include shape-matching activities where children need to recognize and match shapes that have a different orientation or are different sizes. At a center or as part of a lesson, this can be done on paper or with the actual pieces to manipulate as needed.

Measurement

Another important mathematical concept to emphasize during the early years is the ability to quantify materials in the world. Finding the height, weight, volume, and other dimensions of objects are examples of measurement. When children have reached the stage of concrete operations (age 7 or 8), they can measure using standard units such as inches, pounds, and liters. Younger children can explore measurement with nonstandard units like cubes or paper clips. Most important, measurement activities should be meaningful and relevant to children's lives. Consider activities like weighing the class pet, finding the dimensions of your classroom or the playground equipment, and discovering how many drops of water from an eyedropper will fit on a penny (also a great fine motor exercise). Have children estimate before they do these exercises to extend math thinking.

How Big Is a Foot?

Supply pairs of students with a 12-inch ruler, a pencil, and a clipboard with a piece of unlined paper divided into two columns, one labeled *longer than a foot* and one labeled *shorter than a foot*. Ask student pairs to travel the room, looking for objects that fit into both categories. In turn, each student can hold up the ruler, determine (with help from her partner) which label the object fits under, and quickly draw it or write its name in the appropriate column. Call students together after a few minutes and discuss the objects found and the students' results.

Cover Up

Find two flat objects that are the same thing but in different sizes, like two books. Have children cover them with Unifix cubes or something similar and count how many cubes it takes to cover each one. The main idea here is that even though both are books, they can be very different in length, width, area, and perimeter. (Familiarize children with these terms by using them often, but be sure they have a clear understanding of what each word means.) Similarly, you can give each student a small plastic cup of paper clips, bingo chips, or tiles. Allow students to choose objects in the room they want to measure with their materials, such as the length of a desktop or pencil, or the width of a book or chair seat. Also encourage students to use the items in their cups to measure the areas or perimeters of small objects such as a crayon box.

It's About Time!

Measurement is not just about inches and feet; it's also about the passage of time and how we measure it (hours, days, weeks, months, seasons). Besides measuring the passage of time, use daily calendar time to help you teach almost every other math concept necessary for strong mathematical thinking. Since you do it every day, the repeated exposure is built right in. A 10- to 15-minute calendar session will provide the reinforcement students need for long-term retention.

Help Kids Measure Up

Include opportunities for measuring in other daily routines by having children:

* Refill food and water supplies for classroom pets (and chart how much they eat and drink).

* Use timers to help take turns, such as when working on the computer or sharing popular toys.

* Check a rain gauge or thermometer, compare to yesterday's results, and report to the class.

* Use a stopwatch or timer for relay races and other games.

* Use measuring tools in dramatic play, such as a trundle wheel, eyedropper, balance, and clock.

* Play with clear plastic containers at a sand or water table.

* Predict and prove (with your help): "Can two tablespoons of finger paint cover your paper? What do you predict?"

* Chart their guesses and findings about the weight, length, or height of things. Do they notice changes in their accuracy?

* Create scale models of objects from clay, wood scraps, boxes, or papier-mâché.

* Compare objects in the classroom and daily routines to explore concepts such as wide/narrow, heavy/light, far/near, now/later.

* Experiment to answer questions such as, "Do all lunch boxes hold the same amount of stuff?" "How much does the paper we are recycling weigh?"

* Survey adults about what they measure at home and on their jobs.

Where Should Kids Be?

Assessment Checklist – 4 years

	Yes	No
Understands that numbers represent how many		
Represents numbers up to 5 using finger patterns		
Orally names the next number, up to 9		
Counts accurately to 10 orally		
Distributes an even number of objects (up to 10) equally between two people		
Understands quantity growth: adding more sand to the pile makes it bigger		
Uses some comparative language such as taller, shorter, longer, fatter		
Recognizes the digits 1 to 9		
Counts out 10 objects		
Makes reasonable estimates of numbers of objects in a group up to 5		
Understands first and last		
Recognizes and names basic shapes		
Combines shapes to make pictures		
Orients objects correctly		
Understands that different-sized containers can hold different amounts		
Understands time concepts like night/day and the seasons		
Recognizes simple patterns		
Sorts objects using one attribute		
Begins to understand the language of probability: certain, unlikely		
Begins to add and subtract numbers to 4 with concrete objects		

Additional Notes

_____

_____

_____

Assessment Checklist - 5 years

	Yes	No
Begins to count forward from numbers besides 1		
Reads simple graphs		
Counts out 20 objects accurately		
Uses pattern recognition to improve efficiency in counting		
Represents numbers to 10 with fingers		
Understands that a group of 10 is 10, no matter what the object (rocks, dolls, coins)		
Begins developing strategies to solve addition and subtraction problems		
Uses piece of string (for example) to measure objects		
Makes reasonable comparisons (the book is shorter than my arm)		
Compares objects by attributes		
Understands time concepts such as yesterday, today, tomorrow		
Identifies which of two numbers is larger		
Sorts objects based on more than one attribute		
Counts by rote to 20		
Names number before, up to 10		
Makes reasonable estimates up to 10		
Begins to understand that numbers later in sequence are larger		
Recognizes numbers to 20		
Matches shapes with different sizes and orientations		
Creates drawings using many forms		
Begins to create structures with symmetry		
Uses comparative language accurately and widely		
Uses nonstandard units of measure laid end to end		

Additional Notes

_____

_____

_____

Assessment Checklist – 6 years

	Yes	No
Uses a variety of strategies to solve addition and subtraction problems		
Counts backward from 20		
Combines two shapes to make a new one		
Follows directions for moving around the room		
Begins to see patterns in rote counting and uses them to further own counting		
Names number before and after, up to 29, easily		
Counts to 100 by tens		
Makes reasonable estimates in collections of objects, up to 50		
Determines which neighboring number is more, up to 99		
Uses symbolic representations of a spoken number (tally marks, for example)		
Uses ordinal number terms through ninth		
Recognizes that part of something is less than the whole		
Reads numbers up to 99		
Writes two-digit numbers accurately		
Recognizes shapes in any orientation		
Finds shapes hidden within other shapes		
Understands concepts of time in a more refined way (knows an event is close to happening)		
Understands conservation (number remains the same even if appearance is altered)		
Can translate simple word problems, given verbally, into number equations		
Beginning to understand other names for a number		
Understands language of probability		
Learning simple number partners or complements (5 and 4 make 9)		

Additional Notes

_____

_____

_____

Assessment Checklist – 7 years

	Yes	No
Has increased ability to solve problems mentally		
Uses simple standard units of measure		
Uses repeating patterns to count to 100		
Can name the number after, into the 100s (what comes after 157?)		
Counts to 100 by fives orally and counts objects by fives		
Counts to 20 by twos and counts objects by twos		
Makes reasonable estimates of items in a collection, up to 100		
Uses greater than, less than, and equal to correctly		
Estimates answers to addition word problems		
Counts down to subtract		
Translates word problems into number sentences easily and vice versa		
Is learning more complex number partners (30 + 10 = 40)		
Reads multidigit numbers, up to 999		
Represents 100 in different forms		
Begins to understand place value of ones and tens		
Begins to divide by sharing equally between 4 people with concrete examples		
Uses fractional labels for ½ and ¼		
Solves repeated addition problems		
Recognizes complex shapes (trapezoid, rhombus) in any size or orientation		
Manipulates shapes to show congruency		
Can create new shapes by breaking apart two-dimensional shapes (a cracker into 2 triangles)		
Uses estimation procedures, such as rounding		
Begins to recognize complex or growing patterns: +1, +2, +3 . . .		

Additional Notes

_____

_____

_____

Assessment Checklist – 8 years

	Yes	No
Counts to 1,000		
Applies many strategies when solving problems, without prompting		
Understands early multiplication concepts		
Comfortable with terms of estimation such as between, closer to		
Makes reasonable estimate of number of items in a collection, to 1,000		
Mentally determines proximity of numbers (300 is closer to 200 than it is to 700)		
Uses ordinal numbers up to twenty-ninth		
Solves missing addend and subtrahend problems: $17 - ? = 9$		
Writes numbers to 999		
Understands place value concepts, such as 1,000 = 10 hundreds		
Can compare basic fractions with concrete representations		
Solves repeated addition problems mentally		
Creates shapes from verbal directions		
Identifies and counts sides and angles of shapes		
Can make a map of familiar areas		
Uses coordinates to identify location		
Measures area and perimeter of an object		
Determines best measuring tool for each instance		
Fully recognizes regularities in events, designs, sets of numbers		
Recognizes complex or growing patterns		
Understands additive/subtractive identity (you didn't add/take away anything, so it's still the same)		
Understands and uses commutative property of addition (add the numbers in any order; the sum will be the same)		
Renames numbers for purposes of trading		
Organizes, describes, and interprets data through different types of graphs		

Additional Notes

Dear Parent/Guardian,

You may feel that the math your child is learning at school is different from how you were taught, or that math was not your best subject, and you may be right on both counts. However, you can still help your child excel in mathematics. Use some or all of the ideas here to highlight the importance of math and help your child learn and enjoy using mathematical ideas every day.

- Talk with your child about the number, shape, and size of things in games, pictures, rhymes, stories, at home, and at the supermarket.

- Point out numbers in magazines and books, and on signs and packaging. Talk about how numbers help us know how to find things (aisle 4 for toys, for example), how much items cost, how many are in a container, and a lot more.

- Look for opportunities for your child to sort, organize, and count collections of things like clothes, toys, books, shells, rocks, and birthday candles.

- When traveling, play games in the car, such as, "Let's count all the blue cars we see on our way to school." "Let's see how many different-shaped signs we can find."

- When your child asks, "How long will it take to get there?" you might answer, "It will take about the same time as it takes to (... get to school, watch Sesame Street, etc.).

- Go for a walk together. Point out house numbers and ask your child, "What number do you think the next house will be? Will it be an odd or even number?"

- Talk about similarities and differences your child notices in houses or buildings in your neighborhood (number of floors, shape of the building, length of driveway, number of windows on front, and so on). Watch for numbers on posters, buses, cars, and road signs.

- When you're relaxing in front of the TV in the evening, ask your child, "What time does your favorite program start? What time is it now? Do we have enough time to read this book before it begins?"

- When you're cooking a meal, involve your child in deciding how much food to prepare: "Are there enough rolls for us to each have one? How many knives and forks will we need to set the table? Which glass will hold the most juice?"

(continued)

- At the supermarket, ask your child how many numbers he or she can spot. Your child will enjoy looking for labels or price tags that contain the same number as his or her age. Have your child count items in the cart as each one is added, and ask your child to compare items: Which can is bigger/smaller? Which box is heavier/lighter? Compare similar items with your child and talk about small, medium, and large. For example, if you buy an apple, orange, and grapefruit, discuss these terms and ask your child to tell you which is the biggest, smallest, lightest, and heaviest.

- Play games with your child that involve using dice and counters, like Chutes and Ladders.

- Make building blocks out of egg cartons, cereal boxes, or wood scraps.

- Help children learn to solve problems and learn about shapes, sizes, and colors by giving them puzzles to complete.

- Talk about any math work your child brings home from school.

Most important, you want to make math fun for your child. But watch out—you might even enjoy it too!

Sincerely,

Reproducibles

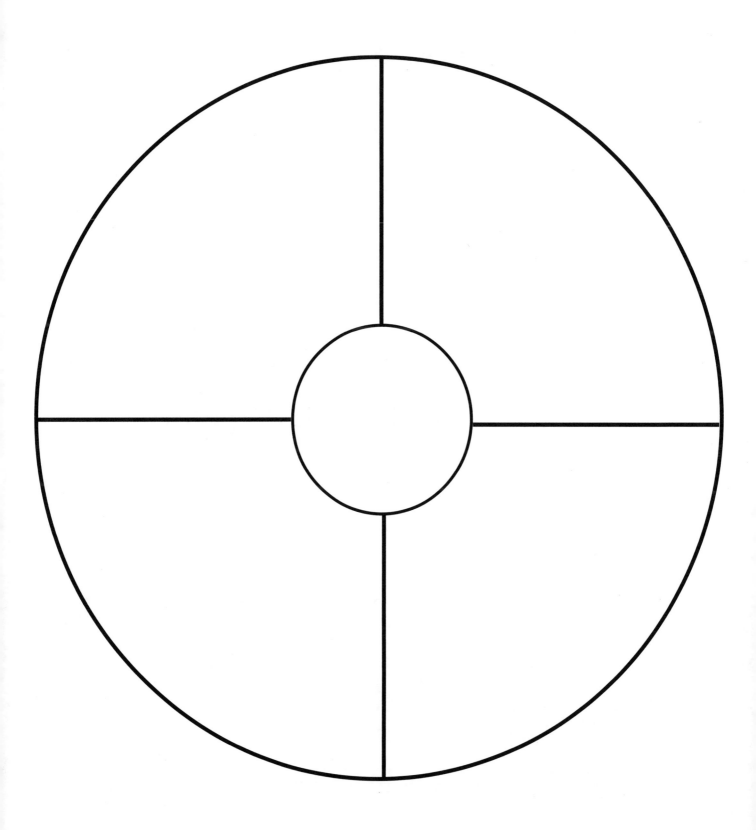

Reproducible for Ready, Set, Action (page 9) and Wheel of Words (page 38)

String 15 beads onto the shoelace, and then take them off 1 at a time.

Place 20 marbles in the cup, 1 at a time, and then take them back out the same way.

Screw the nut up and down the entire bolt 4 times.

Flip the half dollar (or quarter) in the air 20 times.

Do 25 hand push-ups on your desk.

Unscrew and screw the jar lid 15 times, letting go of the lid each time.

Pick up and release the cotton ball with the clothespin 20 times.

Crumple a piece of paper 5 times using only the hand you write with.

Let me tell you about . . .

Let me tell you about . . .

Let me tell you about . . .

Let me tell you about . . .

Let me tell you about . . .

LETTER/WORD SEARCH

_____

Bank

_____   _____   _____

_____   _____   _____

_____   _____   _____

Big Word of the Week

Name_____

Use the scrambled letters below to make as many words as you can. Do you know what word these letters make?

Read a big book.

Read from your writing folder.

Read the room with a pointer.

Read a poem from your poetry book to a friend.

Choose a book from your book box. Find as many words as you can that begin with ___. Stamp them onto a piece of scrap paper.

Choose a nonfiction book. Read or look at one page. Draw or write about what you saw or learned.

Read a class-made book.

Follow along while you listen to a book on tape.

Tips for Reading with Your Child

Here are some great reading ideas you and your child will enjoy. Have fun and look for more tips in school newsletters. If you and your child have an idea that's not listed here, please share it with me by using the cut-off strip at the end.

- Read to your child often and make it fun!

- Snuggle when you read.

- Don't skip your regular reading time.

- Be certain that your child has the opportunity to see you enjoy reading.

- Read and reread stories your child requests.

- Ask your child to predict what he or she thinks will happen next in the story.

- Discuss and enjoy the illustrations in books you share.

- Talk about the authors and illustrators of the books you read.

- Encourage and ask questions like "Why?" "What would you have done?" or "Who was your favorite character?"

- Be patient while your child is reading aloud.

- Listen to books on tape together.

- Read aloud together with your child, in unison and taking turns.

- Take your child to the library and encourage him or her to choose books to read together.

- Leave out a word or phrase on each page and let your child fill it in. (For example, Little Red Riding Hood said, "Oh, what big sharp _____ you have, Grandma!")

- Ask your child to think of a new ending for the story.

- When reading a nonfiction book, ask your child what he or she knows about the topic and wants to learn.

- Discuss similarities and differences between stories you've read before.

- Alternate reading. You read a page, your child reads a page, and so forth.

- From time to time, invite other adults or older children to listen or join in reading aloud.

- When you read together, involve your child; he or she can point out objects in pictures and follow the words with a finger or pointer.

- Echo read: Choose something fun to read, such as a poem, song, or joke. Read a sentence with expression and ask your child to repeat it after you.

- Read children's poetry to and with your child.

- Make a habit of giving children's books or magazine subscriptions as gifts, and read children's magazines together.

- Always have a book with you! A short story is just the thing to pass the time when waiting in line, sitting at the doctor's office, or picking up siblings from school.

- Create a special place for your child's books in your home.

- Keep a few "old favorite" books in the car to enjoy.

- -

Here's an idea that gets us reading!

_____

_____

_____

_____

_____

Draw 3 things in
the room that are

_____

Write down any sounds
you hear when you say the
names of things in the room.

Draw a picture of any part of
our classroom. Use sticky dots
to label some of the objects
in your picture with the letter
they begin with.

Write your name one time in
big letters with pencil. Choose
two crayon colors you like.
Trace over your name one
time with each color.

Choose a picture from the pile. Circle 5 things you recognize. Use a white sticker to label each thing you circled, and then write all of the sounds you hear in each word on its label.

Come up with an idea of your own.

Write your name. Choose 2 letters from your name and draw a picture of something that begins with each letter you chose.

Write the name of a class-mate. Draw a picture of his or her face. Use the color word poster to write on your picture what color your classmate's hair and eyes are.

Write a list of things you hope to do during your life.

Write a story about a trip you took recently.

Write a poem about something that is special to you. It doesn't have to rhyme.

Write a letter to a book character who interests you.

Write a headline and newspaper article about an event in your book. Create an illustration to go with it.

Use each word in a sentence and underline the spelling word in each sentence.

Connect yourself to a story. Explain how something in your life is like something that happened in the story. Illustrate your connections.

Create a "Wanted" poster for a character in your book.

Use a special pen to
write the words.

Write the words in pencil, and
then trace over them with a
fine-point marker.

Write the words in
ABC order.

Write an advertisement for
your favorite food.

Write riddles and put them together to make a book.

Write 5 things about yourself that you are comfortable sharing and share them with a friend.

Write a review about a book you read this month.

Write a travel brochure for your town or city.

Have It Your Way

Name_____

Toss & Total!

								12
								11
								10
								9
								8
								7
								6
								5
								4
								3
								2

Study Guides

Each of the six chapters in *Catch Your Kids Before They Fall* outlines the research about, importance of, and strategies for developing one component crucial to students' success in school and beyond. It is best read chapter by chapter, starting with any one you wish. Study groups can be fluid, with people joining as a chapter of particular interest becomes the focus of conversation and study. Participants should bring a related activity or a print or web resource they have found helpful.

This study guide offers general questions to consider before reading anything, questions specific to each chapter, and specific actions to take related to each chapter.

Here are some broad questions to consider about the general content of this book and before reading any chapter specifically.

- How can this book help with our Response to Intervention and data-based decision-making processes?

- How can I get information about preparing children for school success into the hands of local preschools or day care centers?

- Could any area of this book be the source of a long-term professional goal for me, my grade level, or the entire school?

- Of the topics covered, which is most relevant to my group of students this year?

- What is my current level of knowledge in this area?

- How often is this area of development focused on or included in my instruction?

- How could this information affect our special education referrals?

- Is there someone in my building who is an expert in this area with whom I could confer?

- How can I fit the recommendations into my existing curriculum components?

- Which suggestions can I use right away? Which ones will take time to incorporate in the curriculum or into my classroom routine?

- Does this topic inspire me to learn more about a particular stage of development?

- What, if any, challenges will I face integrating the ideas I've read about?

- Do I have additional resources or specialized knowledge about this topic I can share with others in my grade level or school?

- Who else on my team or in my school would benefit from the information provided?

- What do study group members know about this area of child development? Have each group member share a piece of information that relates to the topic at hand.

- What does the title of the chapter mean to me; for example, when I read "fine motor skills," what comes to mind?

Encourage specialists, such as occupational and physical therapists, school nurses, and speech and language pathologists to join the group when the topic is relevant. Also remember how important it is for administrators to have this information, as well as those who are providing special services—Title I tutors, literacy coaches, interventionists, and special education case managers. Chances are every one of these people can add something valuable to your group discussions and take away new information that will help students succeed.

After you read a chapter, take a few moments to consider the Chapter Reflections & Action Plan sheet.

Chapter Reflections & Action Plan

Chapter_____ Date_____

What new information did I get from this chapter?

_____

_____

What were two things I came across in this chapter that reinforce or validate what I'm already doing?

_____

_____

What are three new strategies or ideas I am going to try right away?

_____

_____

My short-term plans for using this information in my instruction:

_____

_____

My long-term plans or goals for using this information in my instruction:

_____

_____

My action plan to disseminate information to colleagues and/or parents includes:

_____

_____

Gross Motor Skills:
Don't Leave Home Without Them

This chapter discusses the importance of gross motor skills and their relationship to future success with fine motor tasks (like writing, for example) critical for school and beyond. It reminds us that these large muscle movements are one of the first links in the chain of a productive, healthy life, yet their development has been largely ignored in school curriculums.

In addition, the chapter asks us to reflect on the idea of actually taking a few steps back when trying to help our children move forward. For example, if a child cannot hold a pencil with an efficient grip, a fine motor muscle skill, we might need to back up and consider the developments that lead up to that accomplishment: shoulder strength, trunk stability, wrist and arm strength—all gross motor skills. Sometimes we assume that if we just show Anthony how to hold the pencil one more time, he'll get it, when what we really need to do is determine whether or not he has the large muscle strength to do so. As you ponder that possible philosophical shift, also consider the following:

1. Who in your building would be a good resource for developing more activities in this skill area?

2. What do you do already to provide large muscle movement in your classroom on a regular basis? How can you include more?

3. Do any screenings you currently use (before the referral process) address gross motor skills and weaknesses?

4. While reading this chapter, did any particular student in your class come to mind who could benefit from the suggestions offered? Write a short plan outlining what you can do within your existing routine to target these skills with that child. Could other children in your classroom benefit from such activities?

5. Select one activity from each of the three sections—Building Body Awareness, Motor Planning, and Crossing the Midline. Share with a colleague how you could immediately incorporate these into your lesson plans.

6. Share with the group two ways you already incorporate gross motor muscle activities in your regular routine.

7. Ask each group member to contribute an idea, strategy, activity, game, or resource on this topic and collect them all in a three-ring binder and add it to your school's professional library. If you have a parent resource section in your school library, consider making a copy available there, and offer another one to your public library.

8. Consider seeking help from your physical education teacher to plan games and activities that tie into your curriculum and give students some gross motor practice at the same time.

9. How and when can you use the assessment checklists for this chapter to strengthen your instruction and improve student achievement?

Fine Motor Skills Matter, Too

This chapter brings to light how much we rely on our fine motor skills for everything from taking care of ourselves to exploring our environment physically and visually in order to extend our learning. It reminds us that developing fine motor skills means more than encouraging an efficient pencil grip and neat handwriting, and points out that fine motor skills develop at a slower rate than their gross motor counterparts, so time to practice and achieve the necessary level of development is crucial.

1. Besides handwriting, what other opportunities do you provide for students to build, strengthen, and refine their fine motor skills?

2. How do you prepare students' small muscles for handwriting before you ask them to do it? Have you considered the large muscles that also need to be targeted in order for the small muscles to do their work efficiently?

3. Are children in your school regularly screened for fine motor development?

4. How and when can you use the assessment checklists for this chapter to strengthen your instruction and improve student achievement?

5. How else could you disseminate the information contained in the home-school connection letter besides sending it home? Develop a plan for doing so.

6. Brainstorm with the group a list of the possible social, emotional, vocational, and academic consequences of inadequate fine motor skills.

7. Ask each group member to contribute an idea, strategy, activity, game, or resource on this topic and collect them all in a three-ring binder and add it to your school's professional library. If you have a parent resource section in your school library, consider making a copy available there, and offer another one to your public library.

8. Centers are a great way to target fine motor muscles and reinforce concepts, differentiate your instruction, and get your students moving and conversing. Make a list of the center activities you currently use. Do any require students to use tools other than a pencil and paper? What could you change or include in your centers to ensure that children are building fine motor skills while practicing the curriculum concepts required? If you don't do centers on a regular basis, consider integrating a few each week that include materials that will strengthen the small muscles of the hands (puzzles, rubber stamps, keyboards, etc.).

Pump Up the Volume on Oral Language Development

As educators of young children, we spend a lot of time building their reading and writing vocabularies but much less time purposefully targeting their speaking and listening skills. Oral language skills are the foundation for almost every other kind of literacy skill our students will be required to have, so it's critical to develop listening and speaking vocabularies as early as possible and keep reinforcing them every year. The best news is that oral vocabulary is a relative strength for every child and its growth is not limited to how well a child reads or writes.

1. How can you make families more aware of oral language opportunities that exist outside of school and help them take advantage of them?

2. How does a child's oral language level affect her reading and writing efforts?

3. What opportunities exist each day for your students to talk with one another meaningfully and without you as the facilitator? Make a list and then brainstorm with a partner or the group other ways or times to add these opportunities.

4. The research on oral language development implores educators to use quality children's literature to introduce, review, and reinforce listening and speaking vocabularies. How often do you seek out new titles to integrate into your current curriculum?

5. Choose one unit of study you will teach this year and locate related fiction or nonfiction titles written in the last five years to add to your unit.

6. Vocabulary acquisition is not a passive activity. How does this statement relate to the topics in the rest of the book? What does it mean to you? What might it mean for your vocabulary instruction?

7. How and when can you use the assessment checklists for this chapter to strengthen your instruction and improve student achievement?

8. One of the keys to good oral vocabulary instruction is being able to explain sophisticated words in terms kids can understand. For example, the word *artificial* might be defined as fake or not real. Choose a piece of children's literature you use with your students, and pick three words you consider important for your students to know. Create kid-friendly definitions for them.

9. Do you use sophisticated words on a regular basis when you speak to and with your children? What are the benefits of doing so?

10. Ask each group member to contribute an idea, strategy, activity, game, or resource on this topic and collect them all in a three-ring binder and add it to your school's professional library. If you have a parent resource section in your school library, consider making a copy available there, and offer another one to your public library.

11. As a long-term goal for your grade-level team or your school, consider developing an oral language curriculum. Check your state's department of education website to see if there is already one in place, or use your state's "listening, viewing, and speaking" standards as a starting point.

Strong Visual Systems:
Paving the Road to School Success

Chapter 4 asks us to consider a critical aspect of children's development that is often ignored—their visual development. While most schools test for acuity once a year, few engage in visual screening beyond that except perhaps during the special education referral process. Even fewer schools have teachers who are aware of how to strengthen the other aspects of a child's visual system—most important, visual perception, visual memory, and visual motor skills.

1. How and when can you use the assessment checklists for this chapter to strengthen your instruction and improve student achievement?

2. What are the short-term effects of a poor visual system? Make a list with a partner. How does it impact a student long term?

3. Make a list of the arts and crafts projects you do in one month. Are there opportunities within math, science, or social studies units to do more? Make a plan to include two additional art projects this month.

4. Ask each group member to contribute an idea, strategy, activity, game, or resource on this topic and collect them all in a three-ring binder and add it to your school's professional library. If you have a parent resource section in your school library, consider making a copy available there, and offer another one to your public library.

5. Examine your curriculum for the whole year and make a list of concepts, units, and themes you will cover in one subject area. Use the Internet to find art projects related to those topics that you can include in your plans.

6. What are some materials that build visual systems? Discuss ways you can get these into your classroom or building inexpensively. Plan a time each day (ideally) or each week when students are free to explore these materials. Be creative with your scheduling!

7. How could you encourage students to decrease "screen time" at home and increase time involved in visual play? Implement at least one idea for doing so.

Language & Literacy: Getting Down to the Business of Letters and Words

This chapter focuses on some of the skills critical for becoming successful readers and writers, according to the National Reading Panel and the National Early Literacy Panel: alphabetic knowledge, concepts about print, phonological awareness, rapid naming, and oral language experiences. Keep in mind the links in the chain of literacy development, and don't hesitate to go backward to build the prerequisite skills necessary for success with higher-level skills.

1. What in this chapter was new to you? Discuss how it might affect your instruction.

2. What is one thing you can do this year to get literacy experiences, materials, and activities into students' homes?

3. How and when can you use the assessment checklists for this chapter to strengthen your instruction and improve student achievement?

4. Look at the suggestions offered under "Reading All Around" on pages 66–67. What general thread runs through these activities?

5. Do your students write for an extended period every day? What is something you could implement to ensure that happens? Make a plan with a colleague.

6. What are some ways you can incorporate extra independent reading and writing opportunities into your day? Brainstorm with the group.

7. Ask each group member to contribute an idea, strategy, activity, game, or resource on this topic and collect them all in a three-ring binder and add it to your school's professional library. If you have a parent resource section in your school library, consider making a copy available there, and offer another one to your public library.

8. Does your instruction around phonemic awareness and phonics take place in the context of other learning or in isolation? How can you make sure it happens in relation to other things your students are learning at least some of the time?

9. Do you model thinking out loud when you read and write with your students to show them what good readers and writers do? If not, when could you build that in? Why is it important to do so?

Mathematics Makes the World Go 'Round

This chapter asks educators to venture into the sometimes uncomfortable, unfamiliar area of mathematics. If this subject is a weak one for a teacher, it may also prove to be weak instructionally. Math is not only teaching facts and formulas—it's having conversations that revolve around math and creating math experiences that are concrete, relevant, and exploratory in nature.

1. Is this an area of discomfort for you? If so, do you think this affects your instruction?

2. How and when can you use the assessment checklists for this chapter to strengthen your instruction and improve student achievement?

3. What is your comfort level with math in general and teaching it to young children?

4. Do your students have access to math-related, independent, free-choice opportunities daily? List games, activities, and materials you already have in your classroom that could get you started on ensuring or extending these opportunities.

5. Do you purposefully make mathematical connections with students during the day? Think back on this past week; were there chances to talk mathematically besides during your math lessons?

6. What topics, units, and themes do you teach outside of math that you could relate to math? Choose one and plan to make a mathematical connection when you teach it.

7. Ask each group member to contribute an idea, strategy, activity, game, or resource on this topic and collect them all in a three-ring binder and add it to your school's professional library. If you have a parent resource section in your school library, consider making a copy available there, and offer another one to your public library.

8. Do you have a collection of books that revolve around numbers and math concepts? How could you go about starting or expanding such a collection? Who could help you?

9. Have you ever started a math lesson or introduced a math concept with a story? Why is this a strategy to consider?

10. Is there a time during the day or week when your students have unstructured math discovery time and you are available for mathematical conversations? Is it feasible to plan for that to happen weekly? What would you need to get started and what might your roadblocks be? What are some benefits of a math choice time where students are working by themselves or in small groups?

References

Motor Skills

American Occupational Therapy Association, Inc. 2003. www.aota.org

Dennison, P. 2006. *Brain Gym and Me–Reclaiming the Pleasure of Learning.* Ventura, CA: Edu-Kinesthetics.

Landy, J. M. & K. Burridge. 2000. *Ready to Use Fundamental Motor Skills and Movement Activities for Young Children.* West Nyack, NY: Center for Applied Research in Education.

Liddle, T. & L. Yorke. 2003. *Why Motor Skills Matter: Improve Your Child's Physical Development to Enhance Learning and Self-Esteem.* New York, NY: McGraw-Hill.

Pica, R. 2003. *Your Active Child: How to Boost Physical, Emotional, and Cognitive Development Through Age-Appropriate Activity.* New York, NY: McGraw-Hill.

Sornson, N. 2010. *Motor Skills for Academic Success: A Volunteer Program That Builds Strong Learners.* Peterborough, NH: Crystal Springs Books.

Oral Language

Baumann, J. & E. Kame'enui. 2004. *Vocabulary Instruction: Research to Practice.* New York, NY: Guilford Press.

Beck, I. et al. 2002. *Bringing Words to Life: Robust Vocabulary Instruction.* New York, NY: Guilford Press.

Blachowicz, C. & P. Fisher. 2006. *Teaching Vocabulary in All Classrooms.* Columbus, OH: Pearson.

Dickinson, D. & S. Neuman, eds. 2006. *Handbook of Early Literacy Research.* New York, NY: Guilford Press.

Paynter, D., E. Bodrova & J. Doty. 2005. *For the Love of Words: Vocabulary Instruction That Works.* San Francisco, CA: Jossey-Bass.

Reynolds, L. 2009. *Pump Up the Volume: Making the Oral Vocabulary Connection.* Peterborough, NH: Crystal Springs Books.

Visual Systems

Richards, R. 1984. *Visual Skills Appraisal.* Novato, CA: Academic Therapy Publications.

Sylwester, R. 1995. *A Celebration of Neurons: An Educator's Guide to the Human Brain.* Alexandria, VA: Association for Supervision and Curriculum Development.

Language & Literacy

Allington, R. L. & P. Cunningham. 2007. *Classrooms That Work: They Can All Read and Write.* New York, NY: Allyn & Bacon.

National Association for the Education of Young Children. 1998. A Joint Position Statement of the NAEYC and the International Reading Association: *Learning to Read and Write: Developmentally Appropriate Practices for Young Children.*

Owocki, G. 2001. *Make Way for Literacy! Teaching the Way Young Children Learn.* Portsmouth, NH: Heinemann.

Risley, T. & B. Hart. 1995. *Meaningful Differences in the Everyday Experiences of Young American Children.* Baltimore, MD: Paul H. Brooks.

Rog, L. 2001. *Early Literacy Instruction in Kindergarten.* Newark, DE: International Reading Association.

Routman, Reggie. 2002. *Reading Essentials: The Specifics You Need to Teach Reading Well.* Portsmouth, NH: Heinemann.

Vaughn, S. & S. Linan-Thompson. 2004. *Research-Based Methods of Reading Instruction: Grades K–3.* Alexandria, VA: Association for Supervision and Curriculum Development.

Mathematics

Bergeson, T. 2000. *Teaching and Learning Mathematics: Using Research to Shift from the "Yesterday" Mind to the "Tomorrow" Mind.* Olympia, WA: University of Washington Press.

Copley, J. 2000. *The Young Child and Mathematics.* Washington, DC: NAEYC.

Forsten, C. & T. Richards. 2009. *Math Talk: Teaching Concepts and Skills Through Illustrations and Stories.* Peterborough, NH: Crystal Springs Books.

Kuhns, C. 2009. *Spill the Beans: Beans + Number Sense + Problem-Solving + Logic. Junior Level.* Peterborough, NH: Crystal Springs Books.

National Association for the Education of Young Children. 2002. A Joint Position Statement of the NAEYC and the National Council for Teachers of Mathematics: *Early Childhood Mathematics: Promoting Good Beginnings.*

National Research Council. 2001. *Adding It Up: Helping Children Learn Mathematics.* Washington, DC: National Academies Press.

Schwartz, S. 2005. *Teaching Young Children Mathematics.* New York, NY: Rowman & Littlefield Education.

Wright, R., J. Martland & A. Stafford. 2006. *Early Numeracy: Assessment for Teaching and Intervention.* Thousand Oaks, CA: Paul Chapman Educational Publishing.

General Research Resources

Allen, L., L. Nickelsen & Y. Zgonc, contributors. 2007. *Prepping the Brain: Easy and Effective Ways to Get Students Ready for Learning.* Peterborough, NH: Crystal Springs Books.

Barbarin, O. & B. Wasik, eds. 2009. *Handbook of Child Development and Early Education.* New York, NY: Guilford Press.

Jensen, E. 2004. *Brain Compatible Strategies.* Thousand Oaks, CA: Corwin Press.

Marzano, R., D. Pickering & J. Pollock. 2001. *Classroom Instruction That Works.* Alexandria, VA: Association for Supervision and Curriculum Development.

Reynolds, L. 2005. *Centers Made Simple: A Management and Activity Guide.* Peterborough, NH: Crystal Springs Books.

Wood, C. 2007. *Yardsticks: Children in the Classroom Ages 4 –14.* Turner Falls, MA: Northeast Foundation for Children.

Zemelman, S., H. Daniels & A. Hyde. 2005. *Best Practice: Today's Standards for Teaching and Learning in America's Schools.* Portsmouth, NH: Heinemann.

Index

Note: Page numbers in *italics* refer to reproducibles.